# ★ ★ ★ HOW TO BE ★ ★ ★
# RIGHT

## ALSO BY GREG GUTFELD

*The Bible of Unspeakable Truths*

*The Joy of Hate*

*Not Cool*

# ✶ ✶ ✶ HOW TO BE ✶ ✶ ✶
# RIGHT

*the art of being*
~~HOW TO BE~~
## PERSUASIVELY CORRECT

## GREG GUTFELD

CROWN
FORUM
NEW YORK

All rights reserved.
Published in the United States by Crown Forum,
an imprint of the Crown Publishing Group,
a division of Penguin Random House LLC, New York.
www.crownpublishing.com

Crown Forum and colophon is a registered trademark
of Penguin Random House LLC.

Library of Congress Cataloging-in-Publication Data
Gutfeld, Greg.
How to be right / Greg Gutfeld.—First edition.
pages cm
1. United States—Politics and government—2009—Humor.
2. Conservatism—United States—Humor. 3. Political
correctness—United States—Humor. 4. Political culture—
United States—Humor. 5. Political satire, American. I. Title.
E907.G87    2015
320.520973—dc23        2015015431

ISBN 978-1-101-90362-9
eBook ISBN 978-1-101-90363-6

Printed in the United States of America

Jacket design by Kalena Schoen
Jacket photography: Mark Mann Photography

2  4  6  8  10  9  7  5  3  1

First Edition

*To my mother, Jackie. She's on every page.*

# CONTENTS

# Contents

*** **HOW TO BE** ***

# RIGHT

# INTRODUCTION

*"Lessons are things you wish you learned
before you learned them."*

—Greg Gutfeld, Deuteronomy 23:171 (December 21, 2014
[an accurate quote—I was there when I said it])

It's not enough to be right these days. Especially when you're Right. And outnumbered by leftists who think you're evil or dumb because you happen to disagree with them.

You can be lawful, patriotic, decent, reasonably hygienic, and still be laughed off the planet by media snarks, academic snots, and government shills. Primarily because you're lawful, patriotic, decent, and reasonably hygienic.

Being right offers no protection in a world where emotions rule logic, and feelings trump fact. Bring up an unspeakable truth, perhaps in response to a casual but political conversation at work, and you will likely be condemned as rude, mean-spirited, or bigoted. The trifecta of treachery.

The world is moving away from fact-based debate and drifting into fact-free rhetoric. Whether it's about criminal justice, gun control, or economic inequality, a fact is never safe in the face of compassionate outrage. The truth, people, could use a little help here.

In the modern cultural terrain, we—the sensible—are the hunted. Which is why it is time to learn how to start winning a few arguments. It's important not just to confirm normal, commonsense assumptions, but to actually convert the uncertain. To win over those who want to be won over, and sharpen the spear of facts and puncture the flatulent balloon of sanctimonious outrage. We better find them, soon, before America turns into one giant daycare center for dipshits.

In a war of ideas, the truth is the nuclear option, but only if you know how to load and drop the bomb. If all you can do is keep screaming at the other side, you lose. Because sooner or later, one of you will die. And you'll be screaming to yourself. And then the only people who will hear you will be the pedestrians passing by the psych unit. Trust me, they aren't enamored by your open robe. I've been there.

The country is divided. Not just in politics, but pretty much everywhere, it seems. We have two sides, a ping-pong of shouters and amplifiers, echoing talking points they know their audience will digest with unmitigated glee. A frustrated conservative could simply blame the current malaise on President Obama, his beloved, appeasing academics, and a slobbering, spineless media. Like-minded friends will nod, because you're right.

A liberal will look at the current foreign policy mess and blame it on evil Bush, evil Republicans, evil global warming (high temperatures lead to more violence in unstable countries), evil trans-fatty acids, or evil women wearing sashes that say "Miss Florida." And let's not forget: evil Fox News. At this blame-fest the brain-battered liberal audience applauds.

Meanwhile, libertarians sit back, point, and laugh, and

count themselves lucky they aren't in any position of responsibility. They will always be right, because all they want is for the government to get off the backs of people selling weed. Also, ecstasy and some forms of crank. Who can argue with that? As the old saying goes, "It's easy to be a holy man on a mountain," especially when that mountain is on Rand Paul's ranch.

In this carnival of barkers, how do conservatives always end up on the back foot? Sometimes this is a self-inflicted wound, as when a conservative bungles a simple question about women and abortion. (That's why Todd Akin of Missouri ended up not only on the back foot but on the hind foot.) Meanwhile, the other side can shout at will, and for the most part, the media will embrace the message.

To survive and win, we must do better. This book is designed to show you how. Yes, it's an uphill battle. With the mainstream media dominating the message, we don't need another Akin. We need two Ronald Reagans and a Winston Churchill, but with better hair. We need our Obamas—young, attractive voices who can sell fracking to the Arabs the way Obama sold himself to America.

You have to be more prepared than anyone else in the room, even if you aren't planning on speaking up. (Read two articles on a subject every morning and you'll shine—trust me. It's how I make my living.)

After operating in the narrow, repetitive fields of political posturing, I can attest that confirming your viewers' desires is important. That is why I keep my shirt on but my hair combed. I think it's important that I offer my viewers an oasis—where they find solace, humor, like-minded thinkers, Fiji water, and packs of Camels. I confirm what many in America think, and I think I'm right, as I think they are right, too.

## WHY WE ARGUE

Most arguments are about authority and credibility. All arguments come down to this: You want to say, "Because I said so," and leave your opponent speechless. So winning the argument means the matter is settled when you have demonstrated that you are right and they are wrong. Even if they can't admit it, or are tied up in the trunk of your car.

That means it's important to be right and win not only arguments but *followers*. The whole point of arguing is to defeat your opponent by looking great, without hurting your knuckles or spilling your mojito.

If you're a conservative and you're talking only to conservatives, you're no better than a fish in an aquarium at a rest home. The residents there find you appealing, but only because it's a predictable comfort. Most people have other options, and as long as you fail to reach them in a persuasive manner, they will never listen. They will never even visit. And if they never listen, they will never change their minds, or come around to thinking beyond the information given to them by the better communicators in the media.

Some like to think that yelling the same talking points is going to make a difference. That's like an English speaker

4

yelling the same sentence to someone who doesn't speak English, expecting a different result (I make this mistake a lot in my basement, when I'm there checking on my intern program). Power isn't yelling; it's having the facts and being able to state them logically. And that's what this is about, really: power. Quiet confidence trumps bluster so effortlessly that the loudest voices in the room feel it the most. Every time I yell, I feel like a schmuck.

I don't expect ideological opposites to come around to your way of thinking. You're talking guns to Quakers who are happy to be armed with spitballs. If they hate you, they hate you. I speak from daily experience.

What I'm talking about are truly open-minded people sickened by the years of phoniness about what passes for "hope and change." You don't win them over by trying to replace Obama's bullshit with your own. You win them over by making them afraid to look dumb: just explain why what appeared to them as practical wasn't—and why better ideas are at hand.

There's a reason Jon Stewart and Stephen Colbert are successful. They have an attractive ideology (touchy-feely, TV-drama liberalism) and an attractive foe (clunky conservatives with frozen smiles), and an entire industry/delivery system that agrees with them (the media, minus Fox News). If the Republican Party imploded and conservative mouthpieces disappeared, those shows would dry up, too. We (me included) keep them in business. (Jon, Steve, I'll take 10 percent.)

It also helps to admit that their success isn't necessarily unfair. True, they do preach to a passive, emasculated choir. The media loves them, and they love them back. Both shows were wildly popular on campuses, because those campuses are composed entirely of liberals. Viewers are captured in a liberal cage, whose zookeepers are maniacally shoveling ideology. It's San Quentin for force-fed leftism.

But they've also been extremely adept at exposing weaknesses in the conservative shoutasphere. If we screwed up on TV, that snippet will be there on *The Daily Show,* followed by a Stewart smirk. We make it easy; they make it entertaining. We could help them less. Why not make them work for their paychecks? Why are conservative pundits paying for John Oliver's swimming pool? The limey can't even swim.

*Persuasion.* It's not enough to think you're right. To be persuasive, you must be *obviously* right. Like "Oh, of *course*" right. People will like you for making them feel as smart as you are. Making your audience your smart-posse is a great way to succeed—because your success becomes your audience's success.

## THE RIGHT'S SUICIDE PILL

If you want to drive everyone out of the room (and I'm an expert at it), simply repeat your argument in a concerned, humorless tone. We have a word for this. It's called "shrill."

- ★ "Shrill" is the enemy of good humor.

- ★ "Shrill" kills all potential for winning converts, and . . .

- ★ "Shrill" can even make people who agree with you disagree because they hate you so much.

* If you don't think you're shrill, you probably aren't. But just in case, smile more.

You can be persuasive and angry, but anger draped in "shrill" kills everything coming out of your mouth—it's like rhetorical Cipro. And it easily fulfills the stereotypes used by your adversaries. Your anger becomes a red clip-on nose. You become a cartoon, easily laughed at, and therefore dismissed by everyone under the age of forty (and believe it or not, they let those people vote).

That's the achievement of the lads at Comedy Central— they made their opponents the butt of every joke (helped no doubt by the right's own inability to sound smart), without having to express any real anger. Bemusement trumps anger. Because anger is not an idea. It's a feeling. And feelings are empty, remember? And our shrillness helped the Com Central guys along the way. We fulfilled their mission—and then we lost elections and perhaps a generation of voters. Fact is, hosts use comedy to make their point, so they don't need anger. That makes them persuasive.

Mind you, we weren't the first to do shrill. The original angry hordes were the left. And they still command an audience on campuses, in dumpsters, and elsewhere— demanding this and that (mostly that—as in "give me that"). But they get a senior citizens' pass. We don't. So it's time to change.

## A WISDOM WORKOUT

This is a short book with a simple objective: to instruct in effectively expressing pro-market, pro-individual, pro-freedom principles in a way that isn't just right, but obviously right. *Persuasively* right.

The idea for this book has been inside me for years, growing, grumbling, developing horns, like a gestational twin with a vestigial tail. As I was creating the book, I was learning to argue, to debate, to convince, to ridicule. But why did I decide to write all the lessons down now?

I pretty much owe it to my personal mentor and squash partner, Karl Rove. It was just after Rove had been talking about potential issues concerning Hillary Clinton's health, issues that might affect her upcoming presidential run. Suddenly gas filled the room.

If you remember, in 2012 Hillary suffered a blood clot, which kept her out of the Benghazi hearings. "Thirty days in the hospital?" Rove said, according to *Politico*. "And when she reappears, she's wearing glasses that are only for people who have traumatic brain injury? We need to know what's up with that."

It was a blunder only for its bluntness (Rove had only answered a question he was asked, but commenting on Hillary's health came off as "mean," and as you know, only Republicans are mean). The press used him to paint Republicans as heartless bastards out to label a female leader as weak and unstable. The media took this small thing and made it a big thing. Rove should have known that would happen, and was a villain for a solid week. The left partied like it was 1999.

Rove was being honest, but he was far from persuasively correct. Bottom line: folks on the right have to try harder, and they need to learn from their adversaries and employ charm, wit, and facts. It's not enough to say "Impeach Obama" or "Arrest Pelosi." These are bumper stickers, not arguments.

Instead you have to go back to the gym, and get into persuasive shape—on every issue. Terror, health, immigration, drugs, climate change, foreign policy, economic issues, "inequality," racism, women's rights, gay rights, gender issues. If you look at each of these topics, they're potential quicksand and minefields combined (sandmines!)—especially for the right-winger relying on his daily huff of talk-radio rage. There are so many people sick of the liberal quagmire of identity/anger politics. They want a change. But giving them something equally as negative—or creepily old—is like taking away a modern kid's Kanye West album and giving him Neil Sedaka's greatest hits. You won't persuade, and you may induce flulike symptoms.

This isn't a book that tells a story, or tries to convince you of some great idea. Instead, it's about making you better at saying what you think.

Each chapter will focus on a specific issue, and show you how to convey the right opinion, persuasively. I will tell you what to avoid, and what to focus on. I will show you examples of how to do the persuasive thing, not just the right thing. Areas include:

## Economics

The catchphrase is "economic inequality"—which is really another argument for taking one guy's stuff and giving it to others. We should have seen this coming the day they stopped keeping score in T-ball.

## Climate Change

We are told that if you're skeptical of global warming, you're antiscience. Yet there are scads of scientists who are skeptical (like whales are grouped into pods, scientists are grouped into "scads"). They're just quiet. How do you approach an emotional subject like this? With humor, some stats, a little bold unpredictability, and naked pictures of Al Gore.

## National Security

Every government would kill to spy on Obama (many undoubtedly do, or at least try). We need to coherently explain that your freedom is protected by a few well-trained people who do have to do some sneaky things or else your babies will be brushing their teeth with anthrax. Spies have done sneaky things since even before the Pentagon Papers. Espionage really is a zero-sum game; you are either for one side or for the other.

## Gun Control

The weapon of choice for the antigun crowd is rectitude. So if there's a school littered with bodies, and a crazy guy with an AK-47 is roaming the hallways, every talking head will be screaming for the National Rifle Association's head. Nobody will talk about the "deinstitutionalization" craze, which started in the 1960s and '70s, so now crazy people are venerated as kind of offbeat political prisoners, while dead schoolkids are exploited by people who not only think guns are dangerous but wouldn't dream of keeping a nut locked away. Facts about gun control are inconvenient: gun control does nothing to control crime. Here's what controls crime: no-nonsense sentencing, smart policing, permits to carry, ambushes, sharpshooters, and police informants.

The debate rarely changes minds. But at best, you can find common ground so something might actually get done. None of us want crazy people to get guns. Can't we start there?

## Taxes

Is that paycheck yours? or theirs? or ours? When we talk about government spending, is it really "government" spending, or is it "your" spending? Every dime the government spends is, technically, coming from you and me. So why can't we be fussy about the budget? More important, how do we explain that concept to millions of young people who have no skin in the game (but who are plenty gamey and will be skinned alive at some point in the future)?

So, what about tactics? In each chapter, I will show you how to articulate a particular viewpoint, with post-neolithic implements I've learned to use over the forty years I've been on this planet (I don't count the first ten—I was a communist). I use a combination of language, humor, action, and hand lotion.

## Words

Jargon. I hate it. It's the worst thing on the planet (after hot yoga). The key to persuasiveness is executing weasels who employ jargon. Remember, it's only wonks who use jargon—it's their own private key to the universe. It's how they communicate in the media-academic-government complex and keep you at arm's length. Mocking jargon is your way to reach beyond their influence and expose their pretentiousness. And their lies. When someone describes an abuse as "systemic," you can bet your house that it isn't Islamic terror; to them it's "just a few bad apples." But a bad cop taints the whole barrel because it's "systemic."

I also embrace analogies. Give me an issue, and I will search for something that explains it in a way that gets people to say, "Oh yeah, I get it."

I may have an idea that I want to get across, like a bridge over troubled thinking, but unless you're in the NBA, you can't write the whole thing on your arm. Is there one word that can summarize your position, as well as egg on your brain to unleash the information? When I talk to students (that is, when I'm allowed to), I explain that analogies are the easiest way to remember—and explain—anything. I call them strings and tie them around my finger. They're good for getting a laugh, more often than not. And that, as we'll see, matters.

## Charm

Before you can persuade, you have to connect. Whenever I could not come up with a convincing avenue of persuasion, I enlisted my mom: If I had difficulty explaining a "thing" to a reader—be it a medical procedure, from my days at *Men's Health,* or arcane political stuff—I envisioned trying to explain it to her. Not to a child—that's a liberal thing—but to a mom, someone perhaps a bit more cynical than you are who knows the world better, who knows your foibles all too well. You end up translating things from the complicated to the conversational. And if that's not charm, it's at least respectful.

## Homework

Anecdotes are often urban legends, conjured up to marshal emotion. They are also simple space-fillers between introductory paragraphs and conclusions. Your job is to be an anecdote slayer. But you can slay them only by putting the time in and finding your counter-research. Look, you're on the Internet night and day anyway. Just turn off sluts andslobs.com for a while and read a bit of the *Wall Street Journal*—or at least Ace.mu.nu. Which may be on an island in the South Pacific.

## Humor

I'm going to make this point a lot—because you need to hear it. We conservatives need to lighten up, and learn to mock. Creating a joke about anything—even abortion—makes it more shocking, more memorable. And be ready to back up that joke with an argument that is anything but funny.

## Concede

Demonizing an opponent on all points makes our opinion unrealistic, histrionic, and boring. The key to being heard by others is admitting that they might have a point. Give a little to get a lot. We learn this in the first three months of marriage. If you don't, the marriage ends in the fourth month.

## Avoid the Apocalypse

Drastic rhetoric temporarily elevates reputations, but it doesn't help the cause. Nothing *that* dramatic ever happens in politics. For liberals, the end of the world is Rosie leaving *The View*. For the rest of us, life's a rough road, replete with speed bumps and detours, and monotonous slop that passes for progress (sort of like driving in New Jersey). No hall is ever stormed. People file in slowly, drone on, and leave. Fierce political battles happen in countries where chaos like ours is considered their calm. It's better not to throw bombs. Just acknowledge the hopelessness and offer realistic alternatives. That might win over the undecided.

## Appeal to Common Sense

Almost all things in life can be broken down to simple benefits and consequences, experienced in daily life. Imagine if you ran your life the way government did. Imagine, if our borders were the doors and windows of your own home. Would locks on your doors and windows seem unfair? Would you, as our government implies, be obliged to keep your doors and windows open? If someone were to enter, would you be required to house them? Would you have to watch their TV shows? Feed them? Fund them? Offer them foot rubs? While their surrogates vilify you? If this were true, I would've shown up at your house years ago. Why do the sensible decisions we take for granted fall away when we approach greater challenges? Because few frame them in this manner.

So, by talking sense, avoiding hyperbole, and grappling while grinning (which you'll learn to do effortlessly after reading this handy book), you'll also win. And you'll have fun doing it. Which is really the whole point: having a great time while beating the crap out of the other guy's argument!

In short, this book is a blueprint for banter. A weapon in the war of words. A handbook on making the conservative argument or navigating discussions effectively, in a manner that converts people, not alienates them.

No lie, it's the greatest book ever written, by a guy currently typing in his underwear. In a Starbucks.

# 1

# WHY WE'RE EVIL

## HOW TO EXPLAIN YOUR CONSERVATIVE STANCE, WHEN YOU'RE INEVITABLY ATTACKED

This is the chapter you should read now. Especially if you've read the preceding sixteen pages.

As you know, this book is about being persuasively right, but before you can be persuasively right you must be persuasive, above all, about being Right. Because if you can't explain why you . . . are *you* . . . then you're lost. You might as well pack up and join the circus. (Address: 1600 Pennsylvania Avenue. Just look for the big tent and the guy in the clown suit.)

You will be asked why you're a conservative or a libertarian more often than Tom Cruise is asked why he's in Scientology. You need to explain yourself in the clearest manner possible. (I'm tired of saying conservative and libertarian, so from here on in, we're just gonna say "Right." Right? Okay. Good.)

Here is the simple answer to why you are Right: *It is a more practical, generous, and compassionate way to live.*

Now, I'm not saying liberals are impractical, selfish, or lacking in compassion. I could say that, but I won't. Because it helps no one. I believe—and have evidence—that as a member of the right, you can achieve better results in bringing happiness and clarity to this ball of fury we call the world.

Who doesn't want that?

Once you have stated your reason for your belief system—and the laughter subsides—you now have to prove that in fact your belief system is the correct path to achieve that goal.

So, why do righties accomplish these goals in a more practical, compassionate manner?

Very simply: conservatism, enacted correctly, encompasses liberalism. The act of conserving in fact acts as the back door to the liberal heart.

Conservatism is the two trees that support the hammock of liberalism.A liberal heart can be controlled only by the impulses of a right-wing brain.

The left can never lead, it can only pull.

And please note: this relationship cannot be done in reverse. Liberalism cannot contain conservatism. Here are the reasons why.

Conservatism is a set of free market beliefs that helps create wealth—a mass of stuff that then gets shared by those who cannot create it. Conservatism is the baker who bakes the cake that gets paid for by the parents but gets eaten by the kids (the cake, not the baker).

Translation: for a liberal to "get" the assistance he desires to pay for programs and education, that wealth must be created by people who cannot afford to think liberally. The engine that creates that wealth is fundamentally Right. The principles of liberalism have no place in such matters. In fact, even in predominantly liberal bastions like the film industry and academia, profit still rules. Actors and professors still ask for more, not less, for their work. All films have budgets. All colleges have tuitions. We're all evil right-wingers on payday. And when we're not? See: "Soviet Union—falling of."

You do not want a liberal accountant. You do not want a liberal financial advisor. You do not even want a liberal babysitter. In fact, especially you do not want a liberal babysitter (even liberals will rarely hire these!). In arenas where safety and preservation are paramount, and vital to your future—liberalism is never the option. When there is disease, or war, there is no liberal response.

The fluffiness of liberal utopianism fails in the realm of foreign policy. Affirmative action, social programs, welfare—such inclinations do not win wars. Conservatism, folks, is where the rubber hits the road.

Liberalism is a hobby when things are going good. Liberalism is putting a puzzle together on a rainy day. It does nothing about the rain. Here's how it works:

| PROBLEM | LIBERAL SOLUTION | CONSERVATIVE SOLUTION |
|---|---|---|
| Floods | Blaming global warming | Filling sandbags |
| Poverty | Giving your money to others | Earning money so you can help |
| Disease | Giving sympathy | Healing |
| Injustice | Giving sympathy | Reading the law |
| Aging | Plastic surgery | Family care |
| Education | Money | Better teachers/administrators |

Liberalism can exist only in periods of calm. In a country as vast in wealth and innovation as ours, liberalism can latch on like a conservative's groupie—a member of an entourage that finds a place to sleep in a movie star's sprawling mansion, largely unnoticed. As our country continues to invent amazing things that make lives easier, and longer, we can afford to shovel money into pointless projects, simply because we *can*. An entire political philosophy exists, and its assortment of useless overpaid, perk-grifting bureaucrats owes its entire existence to the benevolence of the free market and the competitive motivations unleashed by capitalism. Winning a few big wars also helps (shooting predators allows commerce to continue).

In short, conservatism doesn't compete with liberalism, it sustains it. Without conservatism, there is no liberalism.

## WIN IN THREE

1. Liberalism is a hobby when things are going good. Liberalism is putting a puzzle together on a rainy day.

2. Conservatism is piling the sandbags when the rain turns to hurricanes.

3. Liberalism can exist only in periods of calm.

Liberalism needs conservatism to survive; but conservatism does not need liberalism to thrive. Without liberalism, conservatism thrives, beautifully. However, liberalism is necessary as a reminder that you don't need to think about terror and Ebola *all* the time. Once in a while you need to enjoy yourself a little.

### A Math Problem: Solving for B
Today, most young liberals think A = C. Not A + B = C. They don't know what B is. B is for Business.

And we know business. We know that while a minimum-wage hike sounds good, we understand its consequences. That if you have a pie of eight slices for eight people, and you make the slices larger, then you have fewer slices, for fewer people. Suddenly a pie with eight slices becomes a pie with six slices. Two people get pink slips instead of pie. (Note: a pie slice is an analogy for job, in case Michael Moore is reading this, and thinks I'm actually talking about a real pie.)

So, for liberals to get their minimum-wage hike, first we need conservatives to build businesses, to think like businessmen, to sacrifice their own salaries to pay others; to sleep on floors in order to break even.

Then when they make a profit, and things are going great—when the calm sets in—liberalism can appear and say, "How dare you not pay these people a living wage?" Once the tables are full of diners, and bills are being paid, and you're thinking about opening a second joint—liberalism arrives to demand its cut. Really, it's a protection racket. Sort of like the Gambino family, but without loyalty, job prospects, and track suits.

You think I'm slinging bull droppings? There is science behind these simple facts.

Much study has been done on the conservative and liberal minds. The research is pretty clear: The right tends to be averse to risk, more worried or concerned about external threats like terror and disease. Conservatives—get this—tend to be conservative. They are less likely to play with fire, in just about every sense: financially, artistically, sexually. (Libertarians are inclined to legalize matches for all.) They are cautious in changing traditions (sometimes to a fault), which is why they cling bitterly to their guns, their religion, and that crazy Constitution they like so much—as a brilliant teenager once put it.

You may think there is one flaw in this theory—if the right are all about future threats, how come they aren't leading the charge against global warming? It's because we think, quite accurately and based on predictions from the past, that the threat is exaggerated. However, it's also because we righties target what we can fix, and accept what we cannot. At least with ISIS we know what the threat is, and that it's slightly worse than a missing polar bear.

Liberals are generally more outgoing, more risk-loving, more likely to try new stuff. They are open to new ideas, and less likely to feel threatened by unfamiliar things. This is why, in general, they seem to have more fun. They are more likely to try drugs, for example (which is fine, as long as they don't end up throwing up in my toaster). In short, liberals are pretty liberal—about their own security, their own adventures, their own willingness to experiment (with our money). They aren't looking for commies under their beds (perhaps because they're in the bathtub). Libs take risks that the risk-averse usually pay for, over and over. Which explains the necessity for conservatism. We are the clean-up crew.

Libs may seem to have more fun (and many do), but whether they're happier is an open question. Temporary happiness doesn't translate into long-term satisfaction. The angriest people I've encountered in my life have been liberals (usually after I've urinated on their sandals; don't ever do this to David Brooks—he makes the strangest sound!).

The difference between conservatives and liberals explains why one is more effective than the other in securing long-term satisfaction. One lives for now; the other for later. One lives for the desire to be liked; the other lives for the love of those they hold dear. The liberal son survives off the conservative pop.

If a conservative is risk-averse, he is more likely to save

money. He is more likely to protect his investments. He is more likely to protect property, and advocate for rule of law and preservation of individual protections, as well as agreed-upon authority (like, say, the role of the police and National Guard). He doesn't create a context that excuses looting.

These folks are the people—Asian, Arab, black—who start businesses routinely torched in cities where the leftist reflex endorses such action as a response to "injustice."

Of course, conservatives aren't risk-averse in everything. It's conservatives who have risked much to build businesses. That risk, however, is rooted in fact-based belief (not faith) in the free market. Success is not a hypothetical model created on a computer by a bureaucratic elite. It's predicated on a perceived need, and seeing if demand embraces what you're supplying.

Over time, their risk taking creates a civilization, an infectious equation that leads to building families, businesses, and nations. Which creates more wealth. And it is that wealth that can then be used to help those in need. You need money to make money, but you also need money to give money.

Conservatism makes what liberalism takes. And so when a liberal asks you, "Why are you a conservative?," simply state, "So you can be a liberal."

### SO, WHY ARE YOU A CONSERVATIVE?

* It beats pretending you care about hypothetical injustice.

* It's the only reliable thing going.

* The alternatives exist only at the pleasure of conservatism.

* The women put up with your compliments.

* When the chips are down, it's the only "ism" that works for everyone, liberals included.

* The chips are *always* down, and it's the conservatives who know it.

# 2

# WHY THE RIGHT LOSES
# ARGUMENTS

The left is excellent at extolling horrible ideas; the right is horrible at extolling excellent ideas.

Compare Russell Brand with Mark Levin. My politics align more with Levin, but Brand still makes me giggle. And I hate his politics. He's a piece of hairy dog shit, but he's quick-witted—and that makes him a persuasive piece of hairy dog shit.

Republicans handle humor the way Democrats handle your money: badly.

It makes sense. One party masters creativity, the other practicality. They should work together. But instead they hate each other for being good or better at something they fail to master themselves. To persuade, we need to admit our weaknesses and figure out how to eliminate them. Yes, I mean silencing the most embarrassing among us and finding fresh faces who think Right but act left. Which means for the older Right: who cares if the younger types smoke weed or ain't straight—you're on the same team, so give them a hug, you old jerk.

Frankly, I'd rather hang with a funny liberal than an angry conservative. Because a funny liberal teaches me to fight, and an angry conservative forces me to apologize. My gut tells me that many feel this conflict is all about your age—why look for righties when, sooner or later, they look for you? It's inevitable: a wise liberal becomes a conservative, but needs to dress it up with conditions. "I'm a fiscal conservative and a social liberal," they'll say. Which really means you're a libertarian. Or too abashed to simply say, "I'm a right-winger." It's why teenage conservatives and elderly liberals are equally strange. They both defy the engines of experience and wisdom.

But these days, I fear we don't have the luxury of time. We can't wait for these millennials to grow the hell up. The world's a mess, and it's time we create an army of young smart people who can meet the challenges that we are about to face, and in a hurry. But first, here's why we keep failing:

1. **We have been too successful.** Since the end of World War II, when we helped rid the world of evil, we unleashed decades of relative calm, which gave us free time. That free time allowed future generations to contemplate rebellion as a hobby. Dad and mom sucked. And it was fun to remind them of that—especially when you didn't have to worry about where your next meal was coming from. That hobby turned into a profession—in academia, rebel-

lion became the curriculum. In the media, it became the default stance. In government, it became a wonderful way to guilt people into paying for stuff and ceding power to you. In short, shallow rebellion is the perfect fit for liberalism, for its heroic narrative needs no intellectual rigor.

2. **The left have the young.** Because liberals infest academia like defiant, pierced termites, they're the key supplier of failed ideas to the young minds lining up to feel smart. And nothing makes you feel smarter than telling people older and more experienced than you that they're not just wrong but evil. This includes veterans, businessmen, law enforcement, and anyone who might still believe in American greatness. This fuels all contemporary protest, as you watch young white undergrads screaming into the faces of exhausted, older police officers who are just trying to do their jobs.

3. **Liberalism is romantic.** For the same reasons as above, there is glamour to the liberal getup—and it appeals to both sexes. Women love a man who fights for her rights, even if the fight suggests she can't fight for herself. And men dig the fight because impressionable undergrads find it cool that he's so into the war on patriarchy, while leeching off his parents for tuition. It's a luxury: you can hold destructive opinions without actually experiencing any of their consequences. Nothing makes speaking truth to power easier than a nice trust fund. Again, witness the recent protests in Ferguson and Baltimore:

students come in and cheer the looting, then leave. It's the businesses left behind that pay for the price of the white, carefree undergrad.

4. **The deck is stacked.** It's not news but it's worth repeating: liberal arguments get help and traction from academia and media, who are populated by sympathizers with allegiances to subversion. This means that destructive ideas don't simply sprout, they flourish, and infest the cultural landscape like toxic weeds disguised as daisies. These ideas find nourishment everywhere. The good news: because it is so easy to get a good grade for a bad idea, or to get a story published because it meets the editor's assumptions, their intellectual muscles are lazy, verging on atrophied—after decades of free rein (see the collapse of *Rolling Stone,* a magazine fearful of questioning conventional leftism on any topic from rape to terror). The bad news: If you disagree with them, you will get nowhere in the short term. You will be ostracized on campus, and you will be thwarted at work. It's punishment for being different. But don't expect anyone to notice it.

# ★ ★ ★ 3 ★ ★ ★

# THE JOKE'S ON YOU

*"Most conservatives aren't funny. But most liberals aren't funny, either. Because most people aren't funny. But more liberals go into comedy, so you end up with more funny liberal comedians."*

—Andy Levy, Valentine's Day, Olive Garden, 2015. (He got me a nice Godiva assortment; I got him pajamas.)

Humor is like porn—you know it when you see it—and you never see it in the *Huffington Post*.

Humor is important. When someone makes you laugh, it's because he surprised you with truth about life—a strategy of persuasion that beats an angry screech, hands down.

But Andy has a point—it's hard work being funny, whether you're a righty or a lefty—but more libs apply for that job, perhaps because they're so godawful at everything else.

Me? I'm no comedian. I've never stood in front of a group of strangers and told jokes.

I hate comedy clubs almost as much as I hate doctors' offices. The clubs are cold and cramped and, unlike the doctor's office, the drugs suck. Worse, they're full of drunks who can't decide what they're supposed to laugh at. I admire comics for having the balls do to what they do. I refuse the job description because, frankly, I haven't earned it.

As a conservative on a talk show, I find being funny is more important than being conservative. I let the rest of the folks do that. I'd like to make you laugh and think— but making you laugh makes me happier. How do I do it, when I happen to do it? I haven't thought about it, really, until now.

My simple, perhaps sole tactic has always been to extend liberal beliefs to absurd levels. I push the obvious until the argument can only tip in my favor.

Recently on *O'Reilly* we did a segment on a group of Hillary supporters who were trying to label any criticism of Ms. Clinton as sexist. If you called her "secretive," that would be labeled sexist. If you called her "out of touch" or "manipulative," the same thing: it's sexist. Rather than disagree, I stated that I believed the supporters had a point, and we should stop calling her by her first name, which is Hillary—because, after all, it's a girl's name. Logically, it made sense (if you followed their logic). Lo and behold, the absurdity became real, and when a McClatchy writer made the same case to stop calling her Hillary because it reinforced gender stereotypes, parody became possibility in a matter of days. I'm an effing psychic.

## HOW TO LOSE AN ARGUMENT BY EMULATING TALKING HEADS ON CABLE NEWS SHOWS

- Shout your opinion as if everyone listening is your grandmother.
- Repeat a cliché as though you have Tourette's.
- Adopt a conspiratorial tone (the Council on Foreign Relations told me to insert that point in here).
- Don't do your homework. (It's not enough to listen to Charles Krauthammer and then reiterate. But it's a start.)
- Flare your nostrils. That's for breathing, not for creating space to park two cars and a Jet Ski.
- Embrace ideological certainty as though everyone else but you sees the light.
- Take yourself seriously. It generally ensures that no one else will.

## EXTENSION = FUNNY

It's a pretty simple and effective ploy: sit down and make a list of liberal conclusions, and locate the button that says "push me."

- ★ **Redistribution.** Why stop with money? Why not with belongings—which were purchased with ill-gotten gains? People with money know how to buy things—why should that knowledge be kept from others? We'll be by tomorrow to look at your wardrobe.

I could use some new chaps and a shorty robe to go with those chaps. (This scares any leftist working in fashion, which is pretty much anyone working in fashion.)

* **Global warming.** It's our biggest threat, so much bigger than terrorism, according to our very own administration. If that's the case, consider the amount of emissions caused by fighting terrorism, a less important threat, according to Obama. Every time we bomb a group of rapist hordes, a baby seal weeps on a shrinking iceberg. We need to shift our defenses to battle Celsius, not ISIS. Why worry about beheading, when the temperature "be heading" up?

* **White privilege.** Not only am I racist for being white—being born is technically an act of racism perpetrated by my parents. Not only am I for reparations; I am for super retroactive reparations, which means you get custody of my belongings, my mortgage, my Six Million Dollar Man action figurines, and my creditors. And before I kill myself as my own personal reparations, I will dig up both parents and read them the entire script of *12 Years a Slave*.

* **I'm not just pro-choice, I am super-pro-choice.** Seeing the "achievement" of China's one-child policy, which achieved its goals by eliminating millions of girls, I realize I want that same kind of choice. If and when me and the missus produce a junior, he or she

had better not be redheaded, left-handed, potentially obese, or a fan of Coldplay. If the tests are as specific as I wish them to be (and they will be, in time, trust me), I will make sure to abort the ginger-haired, clumsy, porky brat with horrid taste in music. Oh the choices we'll have that will allow us to eliminate everyone we find objectionable! All we will have left are boys who look like Ryan Seacrest. And girls who look like Ryan Seacrest! If Hitler were alive today (and who says he isn't?), he would jump for joy (or Eva). He'd be so pleased to see the progress his Eugenics program has made.

* **E-cigarettes.** I've read that lawmakers favor banning e-cigs because they appear to look like real cigarettes, which can "potentially" cause confusing conflicts in bars, restaurants, and parks. I agree wholeheartedly and am pushing for a ban on bottled water (it looks exactly like rum!) and Baby Ruths (every time I see someone eating one, I think, *Coprophiliac!*).

As for the accusation that e-cig companies are marketing to kids—who doesn't market to kids? I just read that a publishing company reissued *Heather Has Two Mommies* this year. I love that book! I'm not saying lesbianism is as harmful as e-cigs—I'm saying lesbianism is just as awesome! Conclusion: no good things can be marketed, period—because children can get their grubby, disgusting little hands on them. Personally, I don't think we should be marketing kids to adults. That leads to adults producing more kids. And those kids severely limit our freedoms to smoke e-cigs with lesbians.

* **Drugs.** I love the drug laws! Otherwise called regulatory laws, they're based on banning a behavior that hypothetically leads to criminal acts. Ironically it's these drug laws that *are* the real behavior that leads to criminal acts! Which reminds me of a joke I just wrote: What do you call a drug pusher before 1914? Answer: a pharmacist. (The Harrison Narcotics Tax Act of 1914 effectively banned the selling of certain drugs legally; the very next day we saw the birth of a new vocation, the drug dealer.) I hate explaining bad jokes.

  Taken to the extreme, regulatory laws can lead to the banning of all behaviors that might lead to mischief. And why shouldn't we support that? I'm for drug laws, food laws, speech laws, and law laws. "Law laws" are laws against too many laws, which lead to the creation of law dealers and law pushers who sell legislation on the black market to people addicted to nonsense moralism linked to hypothetical consequences (for example, California).

* **The Religious Freedom Restoration Act.** Whatever this bill turns out to be might in fact allow pious pie makers to choose to not make cupcakes for a gay couple. And yes, despite the fact that we are a country of 314 million people—a country unencumbered by religious fanatics who behead you—it still stinks. Which is why I demand that everyone do everything

that I want. That's it. And that's a belief untethered to religion—thank you very much. Tomorrow I'm going to a mosque and demand they host my wet T-shirt contest.

Or we could just let bigots be jerks and leave it at that. Let the market pay back their idiocy—which basically means you and me shopping somewhere else.

This strategy of extension has been a boon for me—but is unworkable and unavailable to angry or stupid people. The way it works is pretty clear, and you emerge victorious by making your opponent say, "Oh, right, of course." And, trust me, I haven't met a soul who wants to say that to a furious, red-faced jerk.

So if you're one of those overbearing, brawny righties who jump into a fracas brandishing fury like a machete, you'll be the one who's cut to ribbons by tiny, quick wiry chaps jabbing at you with épées made from the labor of warehoused children chained to radiators.

## LEARN FROM JON

If you stop detesting his lefty politics for ten minutes, you can learn from this master of manipulation, Jon Stewart. His strategy: he leads a conservative guest happily down a plank of friendly banter, then pushes him off said plank before the poor sap knows he's in midair.

That's the sad thing about righties—we often mistakenly think that friendly people happen to share our views.

So Stewart will have you on to promote a book or a movie—and then start slicing and dicing. It's fine. It's cool. And as my buddy Denis Boyles brilliantly points out, he never changes pitch—and most important, he never signals the change-up. Instead, in that gentle, reaching tone that suggests earnestness, Stewart says, "So you really believe that The Delta Smelt should perish." This effectively, swiftly turns a conservative into a sputtering punch line.

When you leave most talk shows, they'll give you a T-shirt or a coffee mug. With *The Daily Show,* you get a lifetime supply of rope to hang yourself with.

## BE GOOD

Humor requires good—no, great—manners! Talk softly but carry a big crème pie (a polite one), which is really just an obvious truth wrapped in frothy civility and used to smite your opponent in the face. Jon Stewart has bought multiple houses on that. Rush Limbaugh got his explosive start by doing the same thing: having great fun while dismembering your adversaries.

But as my colleague Denis Boyles reminds me, it's all a fine line. "Conservatives can often confuse emotions with ideas, because they're driven by an accurately perceived lack of respect for their beliefs." The end result: they get mad—which is a state of temporary insanity that really is no different from "madness." Which, you'll note, has the word *mad* within it. It's the opposite of amusing—like Ed Schultz. You don't want to be Ed Schultz. Even Ed Schultz doesn't want to be Ed Schultz.

## QUESTIONS NO ONE ASKS

When Jon Stewart said he was walking away from his show, the media convulsed like a gerbil choking on a gummy bear. Then they raised that familiar question that's launched a thousand meandering articles: where are the right-wing Stewarts? (*The Atlantic* did two of these stories in the same year. Yes, *The Atlantic*. It still publishes.)

It's a great question, because it openly concedes that the establishment media's cult head is an unabashed progressive, and therefore the bottomless love for him in the media illustrates its own bias. But it also brings up questions that are never, ever asked. Instead of "why are there no conservative Jon Stewarts," why not:

- Where are the liberal four-star generals?
- Where are the left-wing brain surgeons?
- How come there are no progressive NFL quarter-backs?
- Why does the left have no Arnold Schwarzenegger, Chuck Norris, or Bruce Willis? Will there ever be a left-wing action figure? (And no, Ed Begley Jr. doesn't count.)
- Where are the left-wing CEOs? More to the point: why are there no left-wingers in charge of anything that requires results? Other than entertaining other liberals?
- Also—where are the right-wing serial killers?
- Where are the conservative Beat poets? (Wherever they are, leave them there.)
- Where is my free market feminist performance artist?
- Where are my pants? (I'm freezing!)

But anger is not an idea, and outrage ends up being a terrible rhetorical device. Only a few people can pull it off. Unless you're a professional entertainer, like Dennis Miller, it's almost never funny. At least intentionally. Really angry people can be funny, but it's at their expense—they just never notice it. But outrage is especially painful in the hands of the humorless, clumsy person trying to wield the rapier of sarcasm (which, by the way, was the name of my favorite *Star Trek* episode. In "Rapier of Sarcasm," Scotty doesn't get one of Kirk's jokes and turns into a scone).

Finally, and really most important: effort is the only thing that really works. Arguments are won by doing the homework that bolsters the joke. Confronting an opposing argument with mockery carries no weight if you don't have a few nuggets of prepared, researched ammo in your pocket, too.

## HOW TO INTERPRET "THAT'S NOT FUNNY"

Saying "that's not funny" to a joke that's perceived as sexist really means that the offended believes the targeted group is too weak to handle something "hurtful." Apparently, you lose a layer of thick skin for every protected class you inhabit.

Recently, Ariel Pink, a genius pop singer, made a joke about how Madonna's last couple of albums sucked, and a female pop singer called him out on Twitter (a majestic act of bravery) as misogynistic. That's where we are these days. Apparently Madonna is too weak to handle this sort of thing. She's such a shrinking violet, you see. But the only thing "shrinking" about her is the one thing she can't bear—the column inches devoted to her rock-hard tuchus.

Of course, now you are seeing more jokes about President Obama, but he already won two elections, so the jokes carry no weight. Suddenly observing that Obama is a joke is like putting your seat belt on after the car accident.

That's the real issue: comfort. It used to be that comedians had as their true role to make their audience at least a little uncomfortable. Not simply to match assumptions but to surprise you. Neil Hamburger is great at this. Even Bill Maher at times will veer off his coastal reservation and slam the left over their cowardice regarding radical Islam. Of course, he veers straight back to the left as soon as the HBO suits raise a contiguous eyebrow. He's like a ventriloquist dummy who every now and then magically says something on his own. When he forgets about the hand up his ass.

It's not a big deal. Righties shouldn't lose sleep over it. Just be aware that when someone says, "Oh, Dennis Miller—he used to be funny," what they're really saying is, "I don't like Dennis Miller making fun of stuff I believe in. It scares me." Which really means: why can't he be more like Bill Maher?

**SOME THINGS JUST AREN'T FUNNY, SAYS THE ANGRY PERSON WHO DECIDES WHAT'S FUNNY**

Let's remind ourselves what's deemed funny these days, by people who work in media:

- jokes about Republicans, religious types, old farts, white men (which essentially are all the same thing, if you live in certain zip codes).

What's not funny:

- jokes about liberals, Obama, women, gays, trans.

The message seems to be: they can't take it.

## THE COMEDY OF THE SEXES

In October 2014, Sarah Silverman posted a video titled "I got a sex change to avoid the wage gap." The video shows her getting a dick, so she could make the same amount of money as a man. She did this video to support the Equal Payback Project. (If she only knew that the statistics she was using to justify the joke were incorrect. She needed a fact checker, not a dick. All she did was perpetuate the myth that women suck at math.)

But many accused her of being transphobic, because transgender people are more likely to be paid less or live in poverty. And so she posted an online whimper that went, "If I literally got a sex change I would indeed find the work force far less friendly. The video wasn't transphobic it was transignorant—never crossed my mind. But to my *unintentional* credit—people are talking about it & so begins awareness."

Ah, yes, her ignorance has opened the doorways to awareness. If only she granted the same leeway to conservatives who make similar mistakes. Those doors are closed.

A later accusation of hers, that a club owner underpaid her because she was a woman, crumbled when the truth revealed she wasn't a paid performer scheduled for that night. Her desire for relevance clouded reality.

The fact is, Sarah forgot that she, a privileged, wealthy white woman, is now a target. Welcome to the club. And I will defend you against the humorless hordes, even though I know you won't defend me.

But has anyone considered the tragic inevitabilities that come with being a male? According to the latest report from the Centers for Disease Control and Prevention's National Center for Health Statistics, life expectancy for Sarah is 81.2 years. For males, it's 76.4. What an amazing statistic. Time itself is sexist! It's anti-male! That's a difference of about five years. Or one episode of *The Taste*.

And it's gotten worse. According to *USA Today* (like a newspaper), "The difference in life expectancy at 65 years between males and females increased 0.1 year from 2.5 years in 2011 to 2.6 years in 2012."

So, let me ask you this: if women lived five years less than men, and it seemed to be getting worse . . . could you imagine the outcry? There would be demands that men *die* sooner, just for the sake of equality.

# THE RIPOSTE

## HOW TO WIN WITH LEFT-WING DIRTY TRICKS

Every battle requires preparation. Meaning, you need to do your homework. If you're not interested in arming yourself for war, then you're just like the people you're opposing: lazy. You're showing up for a gunfight with a water balloon, and common sense suggests that's not a wise strategy.

So, on that note, here are the common smears you'll hear from the left, and how to counter them effectively.

*They say:* **"You can't be serious."**
*They mean:* **You don't believe what you're saying, do you?**
*Tattoo this response on your left arm:* **"Questioning my seriousness is not an argument."**

But what if they're right—and you aren't serious? What if you haven't thought about your point of view enough? What if you're weak in delivery? Then when they say, "You can't be serious," they're right. Lucky for them, they never have to be serious, because they are rarely challenged.

*Alternative response:* **Stick a spork in their ear.**

*They say:* **"You aren't really a conservative, are you? You seem so normal!"**
*They mean:* **Why can't you be more like me, so I feel less insecure about my own choices in life. It freaks me out that I might have made a *huge* mistake.**
*You say:* **"It beats the alternative." Then cradle them in your big hairy arms like they really want you to do. That's the God-honest hairy truth: liberals want you to save them from themselves.**

*They say:* **"Your [political] party is sexist."**
*They mean:* **Explain to me you aren't sexist.**
*You say:* **"I'm not sexist. Some of my best wives are women!"**

If they call your political party sexist, then bring up their bunch: Anthony Weiner? Bill Clinton? Jeffrey Epstein? The Dems have more perverts than my fan club. Very few righties send dick pics, or bite the lips of frightened targets. (William F. Buckley Jr., for example, was never known to do either of these things. Or, if he did, likely he did it . . . elegantly.)

If they continue with the sexist blather, ask them

about Bill Maher or Louis CK, two fine liberal comedians who call Republican women cunts. Be sure
and use that word. So they know you mean business.
I don't think a single right-winger has ever used that
phrase to describe any liberal woman—be it Barbara
Boxer, Nancy Pelosi, or Jason Biggs.

Finally, if anyone calls you sexist, remember that
it's likely a compliment. Women love sexists. They
won't tell you that to your face, but if *Fifty Shades of
Grey* is any evidence, women are sick of hollow men
with no money and no pecs championing the rights
of women to accept men with no money and no pecs.

*They say:* **"Your party is racist."**
*They mean:* **I have no other line of defense.**
*You say:* **All notable KKK members were Demo-
    crats. Specificity in debate is vital, for it
    forces your adversary to use those muscles
    that have atrophied due to lack of challenge
    (which means: every muscle they have).**

Feel free to point out the illustrious list of racist leftists, from Lena Dunham (where are the black characters in *Girls*), to the late senator Robert Byrd (a
former grand dragon of the KKK), to Bill Maher (he
condemns Muslims, per Ben Affleck). The point: you
can smear them as they smear you—using shallow,
lazy arguments, too. Fact is, Dunham isn't racist,
the Democratic Party isn't racist because Byrd was
in the KKK, and Maher isn't a bigot for standing up
against radical Islam. All you are doing is pointing

## WHO'S MORE SEXIST?

A liberal or conservative? Settle this with birth control at twenty paces.

As a right-wing libertarian, you have no interest in their sex lives. You're interested in bonds, not bedrooms. It's the left that's investing so much time in regulating sexual practices and demanding free products. In short: you don't care about their pills, or their thrills. Add that you've never met a single person in your life consumed by sexual reproductive rights who has sex regularly. (That shuts everyone up.)

Then offer them a comparison of ideologies. One posits that individuals are free to make decisions about their health choices (a man can choose to buy condoms, or not); another demands that your choices be paid for, because the implication is that you cannot be depended on to take care of it yourself (you, Mr. Man, should cover all of my options for birth control).

Which one is sexist? The one that assumes you can handle your life, or the one that assumes you can't—because you're female? Isn't the assumption that women need others to help regulate their basic biological functions extremely paternalistic? Who's sexist now? Do women also need us to subsidize pills for menstrual cramps and tampons? Will women pay for men's condoms?

FYI: If you feel strongly about Hobby Lobby denying two kinds of birth control out of dozens, how do you feel about sharia law? How do you feel about burkas, or flogging? What about women getting punished for being raped? Why is your cultural antenna only up for a peaceful family employing thousands—but not for actual death, rape, and misery? I doubt there are many Sandra Flukes in Syria these days.

And by all means, also argue that Hobby Lobby was a human rights issue, in that the most nonvocal minority on the planet—unborn children—might need some protection. That always gets a laugh. Abortions are easier to get these days than gun permits or EPA approvals. There's just no need to force an unwilling party to pay for yours.

out how easy it is to label anyone as racist. It takes no deep thought—only a relative distance from the person you are accusing.

*They say:* **"You don't care about the poor."**
*They mean:* **We want more of your money because you suck.**
*You say:* **The party that's kept the poor poor is yours.**

Yep—all the right wants to do is make money, and then keep it. Which, by the way, is a universal desire among all people, except Belgians. But the simpler response to this charge is to reveal the failures of their own party. And those failures keep blacks down more than does anything the Aryan Brotherhood could come up with in their wildest fantasies. Those who have tried to wage war on poverty have made it worse, through damaging government programs that have exacerbated dependency at the expense of initiative. You want cause and effect: when unemployment benefits last longer, unemployment lasts longer.

The left knows that once the poor realize what works is what has always worked (independence, not dependence), the left will no longer be needed. So turn the argument on them. They hate the poor, not you. Then demand that they clear themselves of that accusation. Let's see them claw their way out of that.

The argument that Republicans, conservatives, and libertarians hate the poor is used as a cudgel to pound you into subservience—to agree to more, bigger government. If you come out against a program—any program—you must hate the poor. But in fact, what you hate is the incompetence of the public sector, and the squandering madness by which they handle your money. What you're really saying is, "I'm not ceding you any more power."

*They say:* **"You didn't build that."**
*They mean:* **You owe the government for all this awesome stuff, so stop bellyaching about paying more taxes, you rich asshole. (Note: rich asshole is actually a struggling small businessman.)**

*You say:* **Look at my blisters. Look at my debt.**
**Screw you, asshole (sorry, I get emotional).**
*You should really say:* **Do you think the**
**government could have created Apple?**

A tried-and-true example of public waste is, literally, public waste: the state of a public bathroom. If no one cares for it as their own, then it's a horrifying place. It's no wonder Starbucks is now the official restroom of New York City. New Yorkers will pay four bucks just to pee into something that doesn't resemble a smellier Mount St. Helens.

*Private* means investment; *public* means "who cares." Which leads to the primary reason why the right cares more for the poor than the left does: The right wants you to have an investment, not just a job. The right wants you to own something, not just to live in something. *The right wants you to care for something, not use something.*

*They say:* **"We're all immigrants."**
*They mean:* **You hate brown people.**
*You say:* **"I'm just for a line. Stand in line, asshole."**

Compassion will always be the Achilles' heel for the right—mainly because we've never learned how to respond when people tell us we're big meanies. And we are jerks. For good reason. Jerks make sure assholes don't steal from everyone else. Jerks are the adults. Without jerks, the world would be a big kindergarten with nukes.

## The Left-Wing Smear Trick

### Examples

| IF YOU | YOU ARE |
|---|---|
| wonder why environmentalists are trying to sell their discredited theories as part of their fundraising campaigns, | a dumb flat-earther out to destroy the planet. |
| think owning a gun in a city filled with armed criminals makes sense, | contributing to a culture of death. |
| think people should be allowed to keep most of the money they earn—even if they make a lot of it, | a greedy, selfish bastard. |
| think e-cigarettes should be allowed in bars and taverns, | someone who wants barmaids to die of lung cancer. |
| favor a border, with guards, | a person who hates little Central American babies. |

The problem with conservatives is that we're the adults—we are the people who say where compassion begins, but also ends. And in a liberal world, compassion never ends. That makes us—and me—the bad guys. But the limits of compassion must be explained, or else there is no real compassion to be had in this rotten little world.

Our lives are constructed simply as concentric circles of concern—like a horizontal dartboard. In the middle reside you and your immediate family (and for some unbalanced types, your dog). Each outer ring contains people of immediate interest—but each outer ring is less important. Sorry, it's a fact of life. We prioritize by locality, and love. The rings work outward like this: family, distant relatives, close friends, coworkers, your community, your city, your state, your country. To preserve those inner rings, however, you must put your country first at times—invading hordes will do that to you.

## The Concentric Circles of Concern

In a debate over immigration, compassion is used as a weapon. How can you not let these "dreamers" stay? To which I ponder, why are Mexican families allowed amnesty and not Syrians, who would also die to be here (and probably need to be here more than Mexicans)? Compassion, for the left, seems to be a bigotry of location—which is racist, since one cannot often divorce ethnicity from place of origin. However, it's really about voting blocs. Mexicans get amnesty because the assumption is they'll vote Democrat in return (which seems odd—they aren't coming to America for dependency, but opportunity). Why do compassionate liberals call Hispanics "dreamers" but not the Chinese? Do Nigerians not dream of a better life in America? The ones fleeing Boko Haram sure do.

A conservative should only operate on taking care of those people we can take care of. Then we can all, together, take care of the rest.

> *They say:* **"You're religious nutcases."**
> *They mean:* **I'm smarter than you because I read Dawkins.**
> *You say:* **"So?"**

First, you need to get over using religion in debate, because there are just too many vying for supremacy, and they all operate from faith. Even the Scientologists and Wiccans have a point—as long as it works for them and nobody gets hurt. And there is no arguing with someone's conception of the divine—it's like a caveman arguing with the weather.

The universality of religion is in fact the best argument for religion no one's considered (or at least, no one I get drunk with in smelly dives missing doors on their restrooms). But that same universality means it shouldn't be a competition. And it's never persuasive in a debate.

★ ★ ★ **5** ★ ★ ★

# FIND THE RIGHT'S OBAMA

2016, for the right, is not simply about being right. It's about being persuasively right. You cannot win without first winning over Americans (or at least the ones who vote). When was the last time we did that?

In a pre-Internet era, some of our current crop of candidates would have been excellent choices. And conversely, in this Internet world of today, absolutely no president prior to Obama would run or win. JFK? Are you kidding? How long before every single rumor saturated the Web? There'd be no Nixon (too weird, swarthy, and mean), no Carter (too goofy and reckless), no Clinton (he screwed everyone on the planet except Sears mannequins, and we aren't even sure about that, because they aren't talking), and no Reagan (too old, too inflexible, and too frightening— which is why we need him so badly now).

Before the Internet, anyone could be president! Hell, even the director of pediatric neurosurgery at a major hos-

**PRESIDENTS WHO WOULD NOT HAVE BEEN
PRESIDENT HAD THERE BEEN AN INTERNET**

1. **George Washington**: wooden teeth, slave owner, powdered wig. Twitter would have eaten him alive.
2. **Calvin Coolidge**: too remote. Not interested in updating Facebook page. Refuses to live-tweet the Oscars.
3. **FDR**: TMZ would run pictures of him in his wheelchair.
4. **Harry Truman**: too mean. "Give 'em hell" is hurtful. Why not "give 'em hugs"?

pital could be a candidate! A guy who's known for separating conjoined twins? Operating on babies' brains—and pretty damn good at conservative political commentary? Cancel the election, and move Ben Carson in, for God's sake.

But a candidate who compares America to Nazi Germany? Or says homosexuality is a choice? That's a problem (sorry, Ben). Before the Web, that gaffe would have popped up, then disappeared. But now everything is forever—especially herpetic flare-ups of cable-ready gaffes.

Granted, the left has been spewing hyperbole for years—and we are just catching up—but conservatives have bigger targets on their backs because the media, being liberal, paints those targets and carries the ammo. We have to be better than that. And the first rule of "better" is: no Nazi analogies. It makes you worse than Hitler.

Memorable hyperbole that lands cable talk show hosts dozens of blog hits is no measure of success. Not even for cable talk show hosts. Leaders must be less Morton Downey Jr. and more Margaret Thatcher. However, given the bottomless pit of bandwidth, the desire to be noticed pushes both leaders and modest TV talents toward the former rather than the latter. They wish to startle and shock, rather than explain persuasively. Downey shouted and screamed—a precursor to so many ills we see today. Thatcher projected substance with a measured delivery that remained memorable without the need for silly shock value. Shock is for those cobbling a career in broadcasting. An idiot can do that. I'm living proof. Thatcher's persuasiveness is the reason the Left is still marginalized in England, to this day.

The 2014 midterm elections were known for a number of amazing things. To me, it was the quiet kid in the back of the class finally beating the crap out of the arrogant bully after six years of relentless taunting. That kid was the American voter, and that bully was a media who protected Obama at all costs. Funny how a left and a media obsessed with the "epidemic" of bullying don't mind contributing to it.

Great candidates won. Jerks lost. Lightweight activists like Sandra Fluke were soundly humiliated. Joni Ernst—the anti-Fluke—won big. (Maybe I am wrong—maybe there *is* a God.) Favoring balanced budgets, federal tax reform, partial privatization of Social Security, Ernst favored bottom lines over picket lines. That's honest-to-God real feminism.

Charlie Crist—that *Star Trek* villain from Planet Orange—was rejected yet again (time for this irradiated loser to begin his late night infomercial career already). Harry Reid was bounced as Senate majority leader. Now he can return to doing what he does best (voicing Saturday morning cartoons as a ghost bunny). Wendy Davis got rolled by a guy in a wheelchair—the same guy she targeted for being in a wheelchair. One of her organizers tweeted that any woman who didn't vote for her should "fall off the face of the earth." The result? Wendy Davis, politically, fell off the face of the earth.

Of course, the biggest defeat—and humiliation— belongs to the media, whose cocooning of their chosen one, Obama, made him so vulnerable. Without criticism, or fear of it, Obama reveled in his own self-regard, inured to the consequences of his own ambivalence. He was the star of the big-budget movie that everyone knows is a flop but no one wants to break the news to him. He was the Johnny Depp of politics.

But in this tidal wave of Republican victories, did you see a trend? Or lack thereof?

I saw one: no gaffes. This was a new party. No old guys saying stupid shit. The press tried to find some, but they couldn't. Sure, the boys at Comedy Central made fun of Joni Ernst and her "castrating pigs" video—failing to realize *that's* why she won. Funny and memorable without being mean, shrill, or shocking—she pointed in a new direction.

The advice moving forward? A tidal wave is great, but it's pointless if you don't have the right surfer to ride the damn thing. That surfer has to be smart, careful, witty, and logical. He has to be the conservative version of Obama—a modernized Reagan—who can articulate great ideas all

## SO HOW DID OBAMA WIN, REALLY?

First he was black.

Historical firsts are a great edge!

(I'm the first sequential hermaphrodite at Fox News Channel.)

But think about this: **President Obama did not have a single new idea.** In fact, his beliefs were no different from the parade of leftist failures before him. So how did he capture the nomination, then the presidency?

**Obama did not throw bombs.** He did not try to shock you. He did not wish to be memorable through reckless moments of unrestrained zeal. Through measured humor, charisma, and oratorical skill, he was able to camouflage straw as gold. And he won. Twice. I looked it up.

**Of course, the media adored him** like an adopted, adorable child from planet awesome—and any opposition to his ideas is labeled as racist, even heretical. (He also humorously indulged the right's most manic conspiracies.)

The successful Republican candidate must be immune to the urge to surprise and shock, while also being memorable. When those two are confused— when one believes that to be remembered, you must be shocking—you lose elections (while gaining airtime at networks). Be meaningful, not just memorable.

over again, as something new, and cherished. These are ideas to be embraced by everyone—from potheads to gays to Haitian Mormons to, of course, Hispanics.

## OUR NEW FACES ARE BETTER THAN THEIR OLD FACES

**Mia Love:** She won—a new face for a changing party. She's black, female, Haitian, Mormon. And Republican. All that's missing is a dorsal fin and an antenna.

For the Dems, she's scarier than global warming and long division combined. The woman is a demographic of one. Which just shows you: demographics means nothing. There are more Mia Loves to come.. I can't wait.

**Tim Scott:** The first black ever to win in both House and Senate . . . is a Republican. Did the NAACP take notice? Well, they did give the poor guy an F on their so-called report card. I assume it stands for "fantastic." Or even more accurately, "feared."

**Marco Rubio:** He's Hispanic, has a bad part (hair-wise), but can talk unscripted better than anyone roaming the earth. He just needs to lighten up a little. He always looks like he's about to complain about his rental car.

**Scott Walker:** Not black or brown, but he has balls the size of Pluto. If he's not in the top tier of Republican candidates by the time this book is out, I'll eat my hat (thankfully, my hat is made of Kobe beef).

There's much to be done. But also undone.

For the Dems, the 2014 shellacking was merely a pause. The big counterattack was already in the works even as the media was preaching compromise.

Yeah—compromise. I love it when the guilty—the losers—preach compromise. It's like an arsonist pleading for leniency because he accidentally torched his own place.

The right candidate is one who understands the terrain—that it's tricky, set with traps, and designed to harm you, while also helping your adversary. Judging from 2014, the Repubs have learned not to screw up. Not to trip. Not to fall. I'm not sure whom to actually credit for this. Republican National Committee chairman Reince Priebus? I would, but I cannot pronounce his name (and I think it's the medical term for a family of rashes, anyway). The next step is actually to walk. Their candidate for 2016 is the most important choice they've faced since 1980. After nearly eight years of punishing purgatory—where every day we as a country were reminded that we were paying some price for sins only our president and his closest confidants refuse to forgive—it's time for a new voice, a new face, a new vision, one that not only reminds us of what we were, but points us in the direction of what we should become.

## POLITICALLY INCORRECT OR JERKFACE?

### (There's a Difference)

In August, Donald Trump was set to speak at a conservative RedState gathering, but organizer Erick Erickson canceled him over Trump's crude comments about a certain female debate moderator. I won't get into the ugliness here, but feel free to use this thing called Google.

*(continued)*

When Trump heard the news he tweeted this: "So many 'politically correct' fools in our country. We have to all get back to work and stop wasting time and energy on nonsense!"

For me, this defense has officially trumped the shark—for it undermines and abuses a legitimate, sound argument. Yes, it's true that the PC movement stifles thoughts and punishes jokes. For decades, many writers and commentators have suffered the attacks from the politically correct—including myself. Hell, my book, *The Joy of Hate*, was a broadside against the tolerati—the narrow-minded thought fascists masking as compassionate crusaders. Trump now targets many of the writers who've fearlessly faced down the politically incorrect. Jonah Goldberg, Charles Krauthammer, Kevin Williamson—they were all there first when Trump was somewhere else. He should love those guys.

So, it's officially time to ditch this "I'm just not PC" excuse once and for all. To claim that you're leading the charge against intolerance, when you're just saying shocking stuff, is absurd. This is just a stance that's comfortable, one that many other conservatives have been battling, far more persuasively, for years. We welcome allies to the battle, but only if they help win the damn argument. The best battle against the PC is brash, absurdist—but also smart—persuasion.

Wiser warriors against the factions of tolerance know one thing: Casting all vulgarity as anti-PC allows nonsense to masquerade as bravery. If someone gets upset because you denigrate a war veteran, it's not because the perturbed is PC and you're bravely upsetting the timid apple cart. No—you're just an asshole.

However, no one is telling Trump to shut up. We're just saying you do not speak for us: especially when you say stuff we'd criticize if it had come from any of Alec Baldwin's mouths (he has three).

You are entitled to make fun of "captured" soldiers, and women and their silly hormones—but do not mistake it for some brave resistance to the PC movement. The PC movement silences voices by attacking intent—whether it's good or bad. The way to vanquish the PC brigade is not by validating their accusations of sexism and vulgarity by fulfilling the worst stereotypes of sexism and vulgarity.

Using the defense that you're politically incorrect when you're just crude only feeds the enemy who wants to destroy you. And for Republicans—when a leading candidate forces you to explain his every careless word, you lose.

Conservatives need a leader who can explain himself, not one who requires explaining. To be persuasively correct, it helps to be persuasive AND correct. Oh, and conservative, too.

## THE FAREWELL OBAMA TRANSLATOR

An unfond look back at the language no one still believed or really understood.

Hope and change = punishment for the past

"We can do better as a nation" = "Be more like me"

"Fair share" = We took more of your money

"Everyone gets a fair shot" = Then we took more of your money

"Extraordinary" = Bullshit

"It's the right thing to do" = I have no evidence so take my word for it

"Now let me be clear" = I'm thinking of something

"Think of our children and our children's children" = Children are great props—unless they're unborn, of course!

"Going forward" = I am running over you

## ★ ★ ★ 6 ★ ★ ★

# DISCARDING YOUR OUTRAGE

Wake up one morning, and before you start reading anything that might get you angry, ask yourself what actually bugs you. Not what bugs your political "side"—but you, specifically.

I realized that by doing this exercise myself, I was able to chisel much of my disdain down to a handful of things—thereby eliminating objects that cause wasteful outrage. I find that now, when I read about stuff that used to piss me off (celebrity crap, Al Sharpton, the *Entourage* movie), it leaves me as calm as the medicated nude strangers in my basement.

So what do I feel is worthy of anger? My chart is, like me during the summer, pretty lean:

1. **Outrage over words.** I understand anger over actions—but not over language. If you get mad over

language, then I should at least get to punch you. Then you'll really have something to be mad about.

2. **Identifying legitimate concern as hate.** If you worry about crime, you are not a racist. If you worry about terror, you are not Islamophobic. If you wish that psychos wouldn't try to shoot up a cartoon contest, you're not insensitive to the feelings of Nutbags.

3. **Divisive politics that seek to create factions to foment revolution.**

4. **Abusing taxpayers under the guise of compassion while falsely demonizing achievers as selfish.**

5. **Misprioritizing evil.** Terrorism is slightly more important than white privilege—no matter what 99.9 percent of college professors think.

6. **Unfair redistribution of slack.** It's why Trump gets nailed for crass language, but Sharpton somehow has power. Media bias effectively manages "the story"; they choose the heroes and villains.

7. **Demonization of those who wish to question "settled" data.**

Okay, it's a longer list than I thought. But here's what's not on it:

### THE LIBERTARIAN'S SEVEN UNCONCERNS

* **Sex.** I don't care who you sleep with, as long as it's of age and doesn't bark.

* **Drugs.** I don't care what you take, as long as you don't try to attack my family when you're on it. Ev-

eryone has a right to oblivion. But you also have the right to maintain a professional high, and an occupation while you recreationally use—or you are just a dirtball living off the rest of us. Please do not publicly inflict your inebriation on strangers.

* **Religion.** Mark me down as "I don't know!" I have no belief in organized religion. And I think arguments over policy should not use any religious text as evidence. I love and hate believers and nonbelievers equally, but I am closer to the latter. But even if I were a stone cold apostle, I'd still admit it's called "faith," which means I have no right to expect others to believe what is clearly marked "something you choose to believe in." Otherwise it would not be called "faith." It would be called "fact."

* **Gridlock.** This is a made-up issue that has no downside other than all of us having to endure regurgitated stories about gridlock. The only thing you need to know is that gridlock is better than its opposite: a group of people wildly doing all sorts of stupid shit with your money (i.e., 2001–2010). I mean, they're doing that already—so any kind of slowdown is awesome. "Gridlock" becomes a calamity, I notice, only when the Dems lose their legislative majority.

* **Gun rights.** I write about guns a lot, but I realize no one is taking your guns away. Believe me: they are *not* that dumb. The real battle is not over protecting your right to bear arms, but about expanding

ownership. The travesty is that, as a New Yorker, I can't protect myself the way my good friend Wade can in a neighboring state (Wade has a bazooka made of smaller bazookas).

* **Government spending.** I hate it as much as you—but it's never going away. It's here to stay—like death, ads for auto insurance, and catheter commercials. The constant complaint about spending is a ruse that allows you to let off steam, so you *continue* paying. The stories of government abuse are funny, but it's better to find ways to make sure they can't get your money. It's not theft; it's *your* money.

* **Liberals.** We love bashing them. They irritate us. But as long as there are teenagers, there will be liberals. And they'll likely be entertainers, professors, and artists. I found that constantly railing against liberal actors is the mirror of lefties screaming about greedy Republican bankers. It's a clichéd reflex that changes nothing. Actors are supposed to be stupid. And bankers are supposed to be greedy. (I feel a song coming on.)

## HOW TO WIN AN ARGUMENT WITHOUT TALKING

The key to winning an argument is to have your wits—and your wit—about you.

Arguing should be fun, and you should make it fun. Remember, the people you will argue with are amusing by virtue of perspective alone, and your strategy is only to listen with great patience and tease out their weak points. Then have fun with that mess. The most important weapon you have is the mischievous ability to create discomfort.

When it's your turn to talk, you should already have considered your predictable response, and are then ready to say the opposite. People hate arguing with unpredictable adversaries. It's like conversing with a homeless meth head. Re-create that vibe (but without soiling your pants).

And, as always, when your opponent is in the middle of making an important point, look over their shoulder as though there's a fast-moving vehicle heading in their direction. (This doesn't work in email exchanges.)

# HOW TO BE A SUCCESSFUL
# MISCREANT, LIKE ME

That's a pretty obnoxious and presumptuous title, because in the universe of success, where 1 is a total failure and 10 is Ronald Reagan, I'm about a 5. Maybe a 6, in heels. I hope to die an 8.

But the title is there to answer a question. The number-one query among most people when I'm on my book tours is this: how do I end up becoming a writer—a published one, if possible? The real question: can you make my dreams happen faster?

(Short answer: Maybe.)

It's a hard question to answer when behind the person asking the question are a lot of people in line for signed books—or to serve me with subpoenas—many of them spending months working out simply so their sinewy frames will catch my attention (which they always do, so never give up!).

So let me answer this, once and for all.

**Lie.** How does a conservative get a job in media, or any-place in general? By *not* telling people they're a conservative. Maybe it didn't matter as much decades ago, but with so much bandwidth and so many buckets to fill, the subjects of politics and of who said what are now actual topics for writing and conversation. Even if you're applying for a job at Five Guys, that manager is going to find your catty tweet on Michelle Obama.

In all my mainstream jobs—*Men's Health, Stuff, Maxim UK*—I kept my views pretty close to my vest. I did so to make sure that all they saw was my work ethic, my professionalism, my good looks. Then when I sold them on the goods, I started to reveal my politics. I was, in a sense, a little Trojan horse. But you should never do this in reverse. Ideally, politics should play only a small role in your life. At work, treat it that way.

But we need to start at the beginning, and work ·forward. Like a resume! In fact, here's mine. Steal it, delete my name, and put in yours. Then ask for my job.

**GREG GUTFELD**
*432 Unicorn Park Road*
*Pegasus City, VA 22201*

*Career objective: To make as much money as possible, date a woodland creature, and avoid sleeping on my sister's floor.*

1. **National Journalism Center,** 1987–88 or so
   *Internship*

**Lesson: Take a job. Any job.** My first gig: I got paid a stipend, and arrived in DC with just a tie and a few hundred bucks. The tie had a stain on it, and a story attached to the stain that I'll never tell (it involved a man, a clam, and a sandal). I was so broke, I had to look for change in sofas to get my fast food (sometimes while people were still seated in them). A woman who worked as an intern near me used to eat cold hot dogs out of the package—like they were celery. It was profoundly disgusting, but economical. The point: I was dirt broke, we were all dirt broke, but I really didn't think about it. (Except when I had a date. God that's horrifying. Ladies, please have mercy on the young man who is neither rich nor supported by his parents. Skip the appetizer. Suggest a cheap Mexican joint. Do shots of tequila.) I was so low on money I ended up squatting in a vacant building. To get in, I had to sneak through a window. I made a border of borax around my single bed to fight off roaches. Amazing I still got laid (it still is, actually). Because when you're young, that happens to you, simply by accident. It helps to have low standards (it obviously helped my dates).

## 2. *American Spectator,* 1988–89
### *Assistant mailroom maggot*

**Lesson: Do anything, anything, you're asked.** My first real job that produced a paycheck with regularity was at *American Spectator,* a much-beloved conservative magazine run by R. Emmett "Bob" Tyrell, a youngish, intense, blue-eyed dandy. I became a staff assistant, which entailed driving Bob around Arlington, Virginia, and getting his car washed, picking up his laundry, and mowing his lawn. Sometimes I had to hit the pharmacy for things I couldn't pronounce. I was paid roughly 350 bucks every two weeks—and I mean "roughly," as in with slaps and jabs. It works out to twelve grand a year, I think, if I'm working this abacus correctly. My life as a writer and editor began in a mailroom, doing odd chores, like mailing out other people's letters. It wasn't my dream job, but I was young enough to understand it was a good job. I drank with Andy Ferguson, got drunk once with P. J. O'Rourke, and met Ronald Reagan, who stayed sober as I recall. The mailroom may not be glamorous, but it's a doorway to adventure and close to the washroom.

The bottom line: you have to start somewhere, and somewhere is never pretty. Sadly, we live in a world inundated by people who make it big fast, when they're young (which is breathlessly detailed by the media). Just remember, however, that studies show that people who peak early decline quickly. Every Justin Bieber becomes a Leif Garrett. Not soon enough, though, actually. The ride down is fast, gross, and smelly—and often ends in a bathtub with a goat.

## IF YOU'RE MISERABLE, YOU'RE DOING JUST FINE

To be a writer it helps to have something to write about. And a few hard knocks give you depth. There's a reason why Justin Bieber's music is fluff, easily forgotten, while, say, Amy Winehouse's or Kurt Cobain's stuff has stayed with us. They're dead. It's a feeling of depth, of experience behind the words. Get that experience. And remember, a little misery never killed anybody (Winehouse and Cobain notwithstanding). It makes you a better person, and makes your inevitable success that much more appreciated. Just don't kill yourself, please.

The mailroom, if anything, offered a lesson to me—one that I didn't learn until a few years later. My first day there, another assistant showed me the kind of unsolicited manuscripts that would come through, and how to deal with them (unceremoniously). "We get stuff from this guy," he said, handing me a manila envelope. He explained that we don't publish them, simply send the reject notice, which is what I did. Rush Limbaugh was that guy. How screwed up is that?

The point: Limbaugh had another job at that time (around 1988), but he wrote these pieces and sent them out anyway. He didn't give up. He kept at it, despite powerless dipshits like me rejecting him because, frankly, I didn't know any better, and it was my job to be a thoughtless goof in cheap shoes (it still is). The same thing happened to me later in life when I submitted pieces to the *Wall Street Journal*. A young editor treated me like transient poop on a shoe, hanging up on me when I called to find out if they even read my already published stuff. (I'd say this overinflated preening editor was *the* David Frum, but it was a long time ago.)

**Lesson: Write anything.** If you're terrified of writing—or anything that makes you vulnerable to rejection—relax. That's normal. Writing is like anything in life that requires effort: you suck at first. Those who never become writers are those who thought they were great writers to begin with. People who talk about their screenplays or novels never ever start them. Simply talking about them is the release they seek. Which is why, if you do more talking than writing, consider something else. Try the pharmacy. You never hear of pharmacists getting laid off, and you save time getting your own prescription.

---

**3. Self-employed;** dates: whenever, who knows.
*Freelance writer*

---

I hated my boss. Here's why: I was working for myself.

When I left the *Spectator* after just one year, I moved back home and bought a cheap computer and went to work. God bless my dear mother (whom I think about every day, as though she never left), who was there and supplied me with chore money to help me keep a semblance of a social life. I woke up every morning and wrote my ass off. I gave myself three hours a day to grind away at an amorphous word mountain. I wrote anything: scripts (which sucked), fiction (which really sucked), and satire (which was actually pretty good).

I found that when I aimed low—short little pieces of satire—my results were better. Realistic goals are less paralyzing, and when achieved are every bit as satisfying.

My first published piece was for the *San Francisco Chronicle* and was a parody of L. M. Boyd's column called the "Grab Bag." I wrote four pieces a month for the *Chronicle,* of which they maybe accepted one or two, paying seventy-five bucks each. My claim to fame is that one piece of satire was taken as real by a syndicated news show. I had created a fake illness, called "Videonam," a chilling disorder caused by watching too many movies about the Vietnam War (I wrote this in the late 1980s when the Vietnam flicks were everywhere). I created fake sufferers and experts, and wrote it like a frightful health piece. To my surprise, people thought it was real. I found my calling. I had an ear for idiocy, and could trick people, enough that they wanted to kill me. Who knew I was only doing what *Rolling Stone* does now!

**Lesson: Talk to people.** One cannot live on a hundred fifty bucks a month—at least not in Northern California, where that only pays for half of a thigh massage (Carlos had the softest hands). I had written some scripts and entered them in contests, but while they had clever concepts, they lacked heart and, likely, craft.

Here's why: they lacked any real-world experience. All were big, wacky concepts—but for some reason, they had no pulse. I wrote from life, and I lived all of it in my head.

I had never done any real reporting. Reporting—asking

questions, listening, and writing down the answers—is key to great writing. Reporting provides you with the foundation for your creativity. Without it, you're just a cloud of words with no meaning behind them. But interview someone—anyone—and you've got a story to tell. No matter who it is. You can publish it. If you listen. So when the phone would ring, I'd pick it up. That's why my first thirty-four stories were about a telemarketer who loves parakeets. Then a solar panel guy called and I had a whole new genre.

**4. *Prevention* magazine,** January
1990–94 or thereabouts
*Staff Editor*

After I had sent maybe a thousand resumes, my buddy Ed told me to try for a magazine called *Prevention,* published by health cops a few miles outside Allentown, Pennsylvania, which later would be rated one of the worst cities in the United States by *USA Today* (and in return Allentown rated *USA Today* the worst newspaper in the country).

I was living outside San Francisco, number three on the list as most livable. Now: a shallow person might ask, how can you move from something so amazing to something so awful? The point is: who gives a damn? You can be happy as a clam in a grim place. And be grim in paradise, which was my current state. (Note: Clams are happy, right? And look where they reside. Not a Whole Foods in sight.)

I looked up the ad in *Editor & Publisher* and applied for the job—thinking that because its name was *Prevention,* it was about fire safety. But, to my surprise, *Prevention* was actually the world's largest health magazine. I didn't know that because I wasn't their core audience: a sixty-year-old woman with cellulite, osteoporosis, or a cat. Or a cat with cellulitic osteoporosis (something I just invented, and will likely have to face someday soon).

I got a call for an interview from a lovely woman named Carol Petrakovich. A week later, in November, I flew to Allentown, deposited into a cold, barren grid of booze-holes and cemeteries. How odd that a grim little place would end up offering me a decade of great experiences, great living, great friendships. I'm sure many people refused the job I took because it was in, well, Allentown. That was their loss. Never let location stop you from work. It's ending your journey before it even starts. So say yes, even if that yes leads you to a tiny apartment across from a graveyard in a desolate street surrounded by ramshackle hair salons and make-believe notaries. The bar on the corner looked like someone's living room. The waitresses at the Italian restaurant had voices like cereal. Hard and crunchy, that got soggy with milk.

At twenty-four, this milieu is useful. It makes you earn every dime. And it makes you clever in matters of enjoyment. Most of all, it makes for a decade of contemplation about how the hell you're going to get out of there.

My first editor, Mark Bricklin, may have been the most commercially innovative editor I've met in my career. Editorial director of *Prevention,* he thought in "cover lines," happily sitting for hours pondering the basic desires of the average consumer. For him, a magazine was the answer key for the puzzle called life. Every month an issue would have maybe ten or so cover lines—headlines that beckoned you to buy the magazine by promising answers to your problems. Sex life? Check. Weight loss? Check. Stress? If you don't have any, we'll create it, just to solve it!

He taught me techniques that were great for getting attention, and then getting the attentive to see things my way. (Note that these techniques don't seem to work on police or prison guards. But try them on your dry cleaner!)

But in order to create a cover line, you had to have a story, and within that story real substance must lurk that you could base that cover line on. If that cover line said, "5 ways to lose 5 pounds," you'd better have five concrete ways to lose the pounds, or you would spend all week answering letters to the editor from disappointed fat people.

Bricklin was the king of the hot spot: a belief that every paragraph in his magazine had to contain one memorable sentence that made you feel like you were handed some form of currency, something you could use later, or if not for yourself, then to repeat to someone else.

Under the tutelage of Bricklin and another great editor, Mike Lafavore (who helmed *Men's Health*), hot spots became my low-carb bread and fish-oil-based butter. Of the most memorable ones spawned from that era, I will always remember three.

"For every single M&M you eat, you must walk a block."

I'm not even sure if it's true—it can't be too far off, I'm thinking—but damn if it didn't get me off chocolate and onto healthier things (candy corn, ketamine).

"The milk leftover in your cereal has more nutrients than the cereal you've eaten. So drink it."

Apparently the vitamins leach into the milk, so you should slurp it down, or else the breakfast becomes a waste. I would rub it in my hair. Which is why, at fifty, I have the locks of a ten-year-old Asian gymnast. (I keep them in a safe under my bed.)

"For every ten pounds you lose, you gain a half inch 'downstairs.' "

(It's a simple optical illusion—the flatter your stomach, the longer your penis looks. This single truth might be the greatest primary mover to get men to lose weight—more so than a threat of a heart attack.) This was also the impetus behind "male grooming" and Magic Mike movies.

So why does this "hot spot" idea matter? Because you can use it elsewhere. I do. Within every paragraph of my every monologue, there is a hot spot—a single thought that serves as an unforgettable truth that sticks to your head like a wad of gum. I try to produce at least five a day. I leave them under coffee shop tables. Look! Here's one! "There is no place on earth where a gun ban has reduced murder rates." I got that from John Lott, a researcher who knows more about guns than I do about cheap wine (a lot).

The key here is not simply to state a fact, but to make the fact memorable—something that sits in your head longer than a burrowed earwig.

How do you make a hot spot? Simply write down the point you want to make, then do something else to distract yourself.

Return twenty minutes later and ask yourself, "Who wrote all this stuff? And why is it stuck to the bottom of the table?" If you realize you know the answer, you've got a hot spot.

For most of us, our subconscious has a better work ethic than we do.

---

**5. Fox News Channel,** 2006 to present
*Anchor, Viewer Discomfort*

---

I wouldn't have gotten the job at Fox News Channel (FNC) if I first hadn't ended up at a weird place called the *Huffington Post,* a persistent rash of vacuous opinion that sprouted up in 2005. True, I had edited three major magazines before that, but none that anyone at FNC cared about. Few of their execs read *Maxim, Stuff,* or *Men's Health.* What sparked their interest, however, was this raging weirdo (me) who was wreaking havoc on their coterie of progressive quasi-celebrity writers.

The *Huffington Post* stint made it appear as though I came out of nowhere. No one knew me. So my writing shocked people for its sheer absurdity, and brutality. My mother knew different.

I got the *HuffPo* nonpaying job as a lark: brilliant writer Matt Labash asked me to replace him—Arianna Huffington had asked him to play the role of a token smart-ass rightie, and he couldn't do it, so he gave my name to her. She emailed. I added her to my spam list. I could have said no, but instead I knew what was important: infiltration, and standing out. I looked at *HuffPo* as a perch on which to perform as a rare right-wing surrealist in a vanity project started by a Greek shipping heiress turned progressive redistributionist married to a rich Republican in a closet (which sounds like a movie pitch, actually). It was a great spot, even if everyone else thought I was nuts. But you must say yes, and embrace the hate and nonsense—for, as I like to tell the neighbors, there will always be someone out there watching. For me that person was Andrew Breitbart, who was running the *HuffPo* for Arianna. We met over the phone, and became inseparable minds until his untimely death.

My first *HuffPo* blog post was a recipe for lemon squares—a splotch of absurdity in a sea of earnest left-wing bullshit. I followed that up with even more bizarre posts—about weird sex parties that went awry, field trips that involved kidnapping, constructing ice cream trucks designed for mayhem, a heartfelt commentary on Bill Maher's graying pubic hair (found it in my office ashtray).

After pissing off hordes of leftists and attracting fans who were conservative, libertarian, and/or perverse, I put out my own site, called the *Daily Gut,* a sinister mess of weirdness that functioned as a storefront for anyone interested in hiring a freak. I hoped someone would find me—and FNC did. I met a guy at a bar (a common theme of mine) and ended up flying to New York, meeting the brass, shaking a very important hand, never washing that hand, then getting my own late night show. *Red Eye* was the first (and hopefully not last) of its kind: a renegade, reckless patch of subversion—and not from a liberal perspective. It was— and remains—the most perverse programming ever put on TV. As *Reason*'s Nick Gillespie describes it: "For years now as the host of Fox News' *Red Eye*, Gutfeld has been the ringleader of the most interesting late-night show on the small screen. . . . As far as I'm concerned, Gutfeld is to our era what Mike Douglas, Merv Griffin, and Dinah Shore was to theirs: a talk-show host who pulls together weird, wonderful groups of guests and forces them to crack wise and call out bullshit as they see it in a freewheeling way." In short, *Red Eye* was *Fernwood 2 Night* meets *The McLaughlin Group,* with a splash of Pee Wee Herman. It was a mess—especially that splash—but a gloriously interesting one at that. I've since moved on (oddly, by choice) but those eight years were the most fun I've had without a shotgun.

## WORKING FOR FREE

Sometimes, doing something for free is worth it (which is what the *Huffington Post,* which didn't pay its writers at the start, was hoping everyone would think). But you should only do it with these three conditions in mind.

- Give yourself a time frame. Tell yourself you'll do it until you land a real gig (four months, tops). It's a pay-yourself-forward kind of thing: I know that the four years I spent doing brain surgery for the Taliban will pay off big-time should I ever get past my squeamishness and decide to go to medical school. You never know what will turn up when you're working for nothing.

- Do not pay them to let you write for them. That's called self-publishing, and it's a surefire way to fill up your garage with four thousand books with the same exact title: *My Life, My Dreams, My Third Nipple.*

- If you write for free, remember never to take their advice seriously. Tell them if they don't like it, to jump in a river of spit. If there is no money, there is no convivial relationship that allows them to tell you what to do.

★ ★ ★ **8** ★ ★ ★

# DON'T BE A PROFESSIONAL

## WIN IN THREE

### *How Pretending to Be Stupid Makes You a Winner*

1. People like helping out those they think are slower than them. Be that slow person.

2. People like pretending to be experts—your dumb questions turn them into experts

3. When you destroy them, they never see it coming.

As our very few viewers first observed, I had no idea what I was doing when I began *Red Eye*. But the best thing I ever did was make that clear. If I had pretended to understand the medium, I would have died. Instead, I treated the show like a basement bar in an Allentown house, where five

87

people sat on sofas and talked shit for an hour, not know-ing about the bodies in the concrete. I was fat, sweaty, and nervous—but never drunk.

**OBLIGATORY TIP ABOUT ALCOHOL**

It was one thing I learned quickly: *never work drunk.* Because if you end up doing better than you did sober, *you will never work sober again.* Performance in sport and entertainment relies heavily on supersti-tion. If you end up doing, say, a great show while high on mescaline and poppers, then you will do mescaline and poppers every day and end up talking like Elmer Fudd. So I never walked onto a set drunk. Perhaps I had a drink or two at lunch, but I was too terrified that I would love the idea of doing *Red Eye* buzzed. Better to be nervous and incompetent than overconfident and incompetent. You also won't throw up on your guests.

*Red Eye* was the weirdest show on TV. It was on a news network, but it wasn't news. It was funny, but it wasn't comedy. It was subversive, strange, anarchic—precisely because, get this, it was moral. It was an hour long, but only on this planet. The most rebellious, careless creature on TV was not a "cool" lefty in a necktie, like Jon Stewart or Stephen Colbert, who rarely strayed from the media's sanctioned opinions. It was the precise opposite. It was an uncool, sloppy, truth-talking dope (me).

There was a method to this. While you have Bill Maher, Henry Rollins, and Janeane Garofalo there to cast in the rebel role as the edgy leftist, in reality they are always surrounded by applause. People applaud them for being just like them, but smarter (or at least better scripted). But nobody wanted to be like the people on *Red Eye*. And people starting applauding us because they honestly never knew what we'd do. None of us did. *Red Eye* had no safety net—we were hated from the get-go, and had to earn every fan based on how well we could walk the wire. In fact, we were hated not only by leftists but by everyone. The hate mail from the network faithful was brutal and relentless. I know, because at times I would call up the most vicious complainers to plead with them to come on the show. Most hated me so much, they refused. It was years later that they called, apologized, and had a number of my children.

## THE *RED EYE* PROCESS

To many, *Red Eye* seemed frivolous and nonsensical. But I had spent years in Clutterers Anonymous, so I explain it this way: *Red Eye* is a three-step process (or the first three steps of a twelve-step process): first it's repulsion, then confusion, finally obsession. It might take a week to get the show, but like HPV, once you get it, it's almost impossible to shake. You pretty much have to freeze it off with a mix of volatile chemicals. It's sort of like a showbiz carbuncle.

Why was *Red Eye* important? Because it sought to per-suade apolitical types that you can have a political opinion without joining a team. You didn't have to be a hard-core righty or lefty. You could eschew all ideology but still engage in "the battle of ideas" or "the kerfuffle of notions." I'm conservative on the economy, but okay with things like drugs, prostitution, and gambling. I'm pro-life but also pro–gay marriage. I can't stand Al Sharpton but I also have a problem with Cliven Bundy. I didn't think Trayvon Martin was an innocent, but the dude who shot him was a full-on creep. Not everything is ideologically pure. *Red Eye* was about that: the idea that tribalism—or belonging to a team—was secondary to following your gut instinct.

I never trusted anyone who was ideologically pure. It made me flee the left when I was young (and caused many in lockstep to flee from me), and it creeps me out on the right. There is no possible way a conservative commenta-tor can be right 100 percent of the time. Yet I often run into people on my side who maintain that it's possible. As much as I admire my righty pals, they've been wrong. As much as I think I'm pretty smart, I've screwed up plenty. But ideo-logical purity forbids you from even contemplating that. I had a coworker once tell me that he wouldn't disagree with a conservative, and the reason? Strictly because he was a conservative. Even when the conservative was telling him to remember the cardinal rules of social liberalism: don't sit on your lunch and never leave your pants in the taxi. Stupid, blind bias.

I must point out, however, that this sort of lockstep is far more common on the left, because (1) leftism is the dominant media narrative, and (2) the left believes the right is evil, so anything, including lockstep, is permissible.

However, *Red Eye* was also pretty clear in the world of morality: it rejected the scourge of relativism, the epidemic of faux outrage, the wasteful energy of identity politics. *Red Eye* maintained that all behaviors are not equal—and that denying superiority over destructive cultures and ideas prevalent in the world spells the death of truth, and ends in destruction. In the early days of *Red Eye,* we had segments that jokingly advocated bestiality. It was a mockery of moral relativism, where everything is permitted once objective truth is obliterated. However, the uninitiated viewer, initially anyway, never saw it that way. I got a ton of shit. Literally—I measured it. It was two thousand pounds' worth of angry, steaming crap lumped on my head. I sold it all on eBay.

I learned that if you're conservative and make jokes, you're on a hit list that my liberal counterparts never have to worry about. Your peers do not afford you any slack.

Lefty types can make jokes about women, and it's okay. But when I made a comment about the infamous pregnant man (Remember him? He was a she, actually, who was pregnant, and now likely divorced and living with Andy Dick.), I ended up on an ABC News clip, to be chastised by Barbara Walters (it broke my heart). The lesson: I had to learn to be funny and persuasive—without giving liberal jackasses too much ammo. However, you cannot guide your life based on those who wish to bring you down. What you must do is make their job far harder. Because they're always waiting for you to slip.

That is my occupational hazard. When you're a conservative, in the media, you're not just a leper (a leper gets sympathy); you're a leper by choice. You will be hated and vilified and your life will be threatened. These days, truth is no longer necessary. Your adversaries will determine and then pronounce your intent when it comes to issues involving race or gender—which means you will be even a greater target when you expose their phony bullshit in those particular areas. If you call them on the debunked study on campus rape, they will say you are pro-rape. That's how they work.

## The Smear

### What Will Be Said About You, the Moment You Break from the Herd

| WHEN YOU SAY | THEY WILL SAY |
|---|---|
| Sexual assaults on campus are exaggerated. | You condone rape. |
| Police are only reacting to volatile situations the best they can. | You condone brutality. |
| I think the *I* in *ISIS* stands for *Islam*. | You hate Muslims. |
| I watch Fox News. | I can't talk to you anymore. |

In the effort to be persuasively right, *Red Eye* challenged you to test an audience who might be unfamiliar with you, and to be unafraid of trafficking in absurdity. We were, and still are, unsophisticated—and letting our rawness unfold urged others to do the same thing. Not all of us had twenty writers, great suits, and cushy expense accounts. We had no writers, no suits, and we probably owed you money. We took what Jon Stewart had for a budget for one show, and stretched it over a month. And it showed.

But like *Red Eye,* all righties arguing for conservatism need to be "better" than the left. They need to be thick-skinned and brave. For you will be afforded no mercy by the preening cowards of establishment media. They are a vengeful mob: they see you are different, and they will come for you, because your difference sparks insecurity. It's the biggest hypocrisy of the fawning press that followed Jon Stewart's exit. Sure, he was funny, smart, and good at what he did. But there was little rebellion in his telecasts, little or no risk in what he did. Who was he pissing off? Anyone?

What you plan on doing takes more balls. You're not just thinking your ideas; you're now trying to establish a plan to articulate them in a winning manner, which will bring you more ridicule than accolades. In fact, you will be mocked for buying this book; you will be mocked for asserting an alternative road to this nauseating, sanctioned hipness. And that mockery will make you the truly radical in this sea of lockstep lemmings. Just be prepared, my friends. Once you reject the assumptions of the mob, the mob gets scared. And what does a scared mob do? Plenty.

★ ★ ★ **9** ★ ★ ★

# OUTCOMPASSION THEM!

So, how do you win an argument against someone who thinks you're evil? Who thinks you're greedy, selfish, wrong, racist, and, like I said, evil? Don't ask me, I'm evil (but sexy).

But last week, I was walking with a friend of mine, a real estate guy named Joe—and he asked me what I thought of Andrew Cuomo. I said that I thought he was weak, and waffling way too much on fracking (which is partly responsible for a welcome move toward energy independence). I believe we should be fracking, and helping out the rest of New York State, not just the rich-ass Manhattanites. My buddy then said, "But fracking is dangerous!" I asked him how, knowing full well the information he was about to give me. I had heard it before: fracking causes earthquakes, pollutes groundwater, causes your tap water to ignite, makes you grow breasts that shoot out a fiery spray of milk and peppermint-flavored lava.

I was about to bite his head off, but then I pulled back, and realized the only fault he was guilty of was not reading beyond the *Times* editorials (plus his head didn't look very tasty). He's not in the media business—so he doesn't have to read the crap I read. And he's got a new wife, a new baby. Unlike me, he has a life. So I argued from false mixed emotion.

This is important because it removes the sweaty veneer of ideological excess. While I love it when I'm certain about something, I realize those are rare moments in life. You cannot be certain about all things. As an agnostic, I do not call myself an atheist, because, to put it simply, "I don't know." For all I know there is a god, and it's some dude in Jersey named Ned. True, I've pretty much discounted this theory—Ned has bad skin and a Beatle-do, qualities rarely associated with the divine. But the point is: I can't be 100 percent sure. So I punt.

Saying "I don't know" creates a wonderful bridge to other people. Admitting that you're not entirely 100 percent positive that you're right allows opponents to relax enough that you can pounce—and beat the crap out of them with facts, logic, common sense, and maybe some nunchuks. But first you must let them trust you by admitting uncertainty. Remember, your job isn't to confirm but to convert. And conversion requires some humble pie up front. (By the way, this works in marriage. It's also why it took until I was forty for someone to marry me.)

Uncertainty can only work by paving the path for a rebuttal that is infused with compassion. Meaning: although you agree with them on the premise, after much thought you've found a way that makes life more livable for more people. Your compassion for the planet beats their compassion for the planet.

This is key: the left's primary argument is based on the notion "you don't care." But you do. So rather than immediately grant them that territory, take it from them at the start. Show them that you care so much, you can't possibly agree with them.

---

**HOW DO YOU CARE?**

1. You're so green you think the environment groups are all in cahoots with the oil companies. Don't trust them.
2. Windmills are agents of the bird holocaust, killing billions of our avian brothers and sisters every year without the dignity of a good brining.
3. If you're against global warming, you want old people to freeze to death. Which sucks because old people are great! And definitely better unfrozen.
4. I would ban coal, but I fear my white privilege is making me hate something only because it's black.

---

## Example One: Fracking

So, back to Joe: I pull him gently over to my side by telling him that I too hate polluters and calculating oil companies out to make a buck. But then . . .

"That's the weird thing about fracking, Joe: What are we fracking? *Natural* gas. That's why I am for it. I am pro-environment, and most environmentalists were for natural gas because it was natural. Natural gas *was* the alternative to all those dirty fuels." Then I explain that environmentalists changed their tune as we found better ways to access it. So the only difference among environmentalists, before the boom and after—was the boom: we found more of this amazing clean fuel. In short, the greenie would be for fracking, if we did less of it.

It's an interesting question, why so many greenies were for natural gas and now are against it. It makes me think they're only for something that doesn't work! (Must be why so many are Cubs fans.) My gut tells me once we figure out if solar power can deliver real energy, they'll come out against that, too (the sun is bigoted against the Irish).

## Example Two: Climate Change

Of course, the climate is changing. It always has, and always will. There have been ice ages followed by warming periods, and vice versa—and this happened well before the arrival of the smokestack, the SUV, the Pajama Jean. Hell, my *personal* climate changes several times a day. If that sounds good to you, get in touch.

That doesn't mean you should ignore data. You're intrigued and fascinated by climate models—in fact, they worry the hell out of you. Yes, they worry you. Until you are always relieved when they turn out to be *wrong*! And you hope that they continue to be wrong. You're watching it closely—because you care even more than they do! Even more than Al Gore and George Clooney! You weep nightly for nature, and soil yourself every morning in solidarity with the earth.

Then add that while you believe wholeheartedly in protecting the environment, it would be foolish to hand money over to people who think they have *the Solution.*

It's not just antiscience, it's anti–common sense. If you wouldn't hand your money over to a huckster who promises you'll stop aging if you just use his magical elixir, in a plain brown wrapper (I finally learned), why would you do the same with climate change? Explain that gullibility is amusing only when it's other people's money being squandered. (If you really want to lay it on, you can add that that money could be better spent building low-income housing.)

Most important: you must tell them that you hope that there is *some* climate change, for subtle increases in temperature can actually benefit the planet by making it more hospitable for growth of plants and vegetables. The warmer, the better. That's science, as told by death. Just a one-degree uptick and we'll all have beautiful tomatoes growing in our living rooms!

Finally, you can agree that while coal seems dirty, to try to ban it is selfish, evil, and reeks of white privilege. After all, it's easy *for you* to ban it, when you're not in some third-world country burning feces to stay alive. As we all know, there is no force stronger in the rhetorical universe than that of liberal race-guilt. Pin your argument to race and you can convince a liberal to paint his ass red and skateboard down Broadway. Which actually might finally account for some of the things I've seen in New York City.

### Example Three: Gun Control

When a massacre occurs, the media decides *we must do something now.* The mistake is to mimic the NRA and come out guns blazing in defense of, well, guns blazing. It's better to admit that there is a problem (one that isn't getting any worse, but no one wants to hear that). Concede. Compassionately. *Sound like them.* Agree that massacres in schools are horrible. . . . Who wouldn't? And, of course, we need to figure out ways to stop them. But taking guns away from legal gun-owning, law-abiding sane people *won't stop it.* The typical shooter is an unbalanced, fringe loner. I want to stop them, just like you. Is there a genuinely effective way to achieve that?

Bolster your position with facts: that most shooters target gun-free zones; that these school attacks aren't becoming more frequent—although there seems to be a proliferation of alienated untreated individuals (a problem our society used to address); and that armed security seems to be the most sensible method of caring for students (it's called protecting them). The idea of more effective permitting is sound—meaning no permits for the emotionally disturbed.

The examples above show you what arguments to make, but also how to make them. Be calm, compassionate, relaxed, informed. The "how-to" part in the delivery can be summed up thusly: don't be a jerk. You *care.* You're destroying numerous clichés at once. And if they don't return that favor, shoot them in the face numerous times (with a cake-frosting gun).

# ★ ★ ★ 10 ★ ★ ★

# HIJACK THE LANGUAGE

Words are weapons. In careless hands they'll shoot you in the underpants. Control of the language doesn't just shape the debate, it smears the opposition through subtle, sometimes imperceptible shifts. The choice of verbiage can link a present belief to the past, relegating your opinions to a hateful, hellish point in history.

A recent example, from last November, features Brian Stelter, the host of CNN's oddly titled *Reliable Sources,* interviewing Weather Channel cofounder John Coleman. Coleman had made news for claiming that the climate change hysteria is mostly that: hysteria.

Stelter opened the segment referring to Coleman as a "denier." Not a skeptical scientist (which Coleman is). But a "denier." So, where have you heard that word before? (It rhymes with "holocaust," as in "holocaust denier.")

Stelter didn't invent this smear—it's been around for a while. But by using it on CNN, he took it mainstream.

## THE REAL DENIERS

Call a global warming skeptic a "denier," and you link him to Holocaust denier nutbags. But just because I condemn this gimmick, doesn't mean you cannot use it for your own personal amusement.

**Terror Denier:** When President Obama referred to the January 2015 attack on a Jewish market in France as "random" the same week his White House stated that global warming is a bigger threat than terror, it could lead only to one conclusion: that our president and his minions are "terror deniers."

If there is one true Islamophobe, it's Obama. He's so terrified of pissing off Muslims, he thinks modern terror is just an iteration of the Spanish Inquisition. He's so scared of Islamic condemnation, he won't even draw Muhammad Ali.

**Science Denier:** When experts deny the pause in global warming and instead point to imperceptible increases in temperature that can be canceled out by margin of error, call them this. Then ask them if they believe in evolution.

**Justice Denier:** Anyone who sees justification in looting. These are usually white liberals living in comfortable neighborhoods far away from where the looting they encourage takes place. How long do you think your average literature professor would be okay with looting if the looters were trashing his office and carting off his leather easy chair and Noam Chomsky action figures? The more removed the violence, the more they romanticize it.

**Race Denier:** Anyone who denies that President Obama is half-white, or that Clarence Thomas is really black.

**Hygiene Denier:** Anyone who dates an activist.

It's pretty cheap: Stelter portrays Coleman on par with those who deny the Holocaust. It's subtle, casual, and—in Stelter's well-manicured dome—considered clever. But we get it: calling Coleman—a reliable, decent human being who's followed the science—a denier makes him a nut who would perhaps also deny that six million Jews died at the hands of Nazi Germany. If I were in some studio and a host called me a denier, I might punch him (which might explain my absence from *Reliable Sources*).

Liberals use language as propaganda, designed to stain their adversaries permanently. It beats facts or coherent arguments. Stelter could have marshaled evidence, but he chose to call Coleman a "denier," which firmly exposed Stelter's own bias and his willingness to protect it.

The Hitler comparison isn't new. And as those of you who were early fans of *Red Eye* know, at the end of every monologue on the show, I would say, "If you don't agree with me, then you, sir, are worse than Hitler."

I did that to mock that reflex, thereby eliminating that avenue of response. Instead they would have to respond with facts. And if they had none, they just went silent. Or tried to find something worse to compare me to (Christmas, capitalists, bunnies).

## Codesmears

Here's how tolerant people speak—and what they're thinking when they use their own coded language.

| THEY'RE SAYING | THEY'RE THINKING |
| --- | --- |
| Christian | bigot |
| Boy Scout | intolerant, homophobic |
| male | rapist |
| husband | abuser |
| Catholic priest | pedophile |
| pedophile | victim of intolerance |

That's the first weapon in this battle: calling them out on their vicious mindset and insidious behavior. It was something Andrew Breitbart was great at: stopping the path of attack before it took hold, calling adversaries on their little games.

"Denier" is but one example of the left's use of language to beat you back, and down. They hope that by using such inflammatory rhetoric, you will spend more time defending yourself than actually pursuing your point of view. You cannot persuade people if you're too busy trying to convince them you're not a Nazi.

Race is another fantastic tool at their disposal, and often their last line of defense. When all else fails, call some right-winger a modern-day "Bull Connor," which works only if everyone forgets that the Birmingham, Alabama, police chief was a Democrat (and most people do).

I was once called "Bull Connor" by a leftist, and let it slide because I thought it was an old football player (it made me think of Bronko Nagurski). But let's face it—most people do think he was an old fullback. Still, either way they get the inference: redneck.

Mutations of language abound. Usually all of these hilarious, misleading creations are perpetrated by the left. The right rarely tries to alter language, but perhaps it's time we should. I mean, if liberals can change the language, why can't we?

Look how the left has undermined common sense with incoherent, toleratic bullshit:

* **Terror has become "workplace violence."** True, the massacre at Fort Hood happened at "work," but don't insult our intelligence and deprive the victims of what they need to get on with their lives.

* **Abortion is no longer the active elimination of a future life—but a "choice."** A choice used to be soup or salad. Now it's fetus or no fetus. Oddly, even dismemberment of the unborn child is now folded into this "choice."

* **Minimum wage becomes "living" wage**—adjusting what normally would be acceptable to a sixteen-year-old pimple-heavy, hormonally infected cretin like myself in 1980, to something designed for a wage earner supporting a family. It's a nice little magic act—shifting the purpose of something that's pretty helpful for one group of people to something downright harmful to those it wasn't intended for.

  Business owners used to be lauded for hiring kids in their neighborhood—giving them their first job, getting them off the streets, and keeping them out of trouble. Now they're pilloried for not paying a "living wage." It's this kind of horseshit that gives horseshit a bad reputation.

* **"Undocumented."** The fact that this has been adopted in the media as a replacement for "illegal" illustrates the media's overwhelming feelings on amnesty, and also a lack of vertebrae. Calling an illegal alien an illegal alien is so horrifying, we should edit out any mention of "alien" in ET. "Undocumented" implies that if you simply entered a name into a ledger, it would all suddenly become legal.

* **"Militarization."** An old chestnut from the Occupy Wall Street Days, and later the catchphrase of 2014—it was used by various minions in broadcast news to describe the appearance of the police force looking to confront rioters in Ferguson. Yeah, they looked pretty intimidating—but that's the point, you idiots. Scary beats meek. "Militarization" is simply a whiner's description of "very prepared."

★ **White privilege.** This now-popular buzzword means that any achievement by a white person is based on racism. Seeing the world as a gigantic racist plot in which every Caucasian is evil is a form of hysteria, one that undercuts the real fights against legitimate racists.

★ **"Whistle-blowers."** In the old days we called them traitors. But as we've come to politicize everything, including national security—which has dissolved our natural (and necessary) unity against outside threats—people who made our country less safe (Snowden, Greenwald, WikiLeaks, Chelsea Manning) are portrayed as heroes. Or "whistle-blowers." But who exactly are they blowing the whistle on? Probably the only sane country left on this planet.

★ **"Overseas contingency operation."** Their most tortured locution. Write in with the correct definition of that on a cocktail napkin and I will send you a eight-by-ten illustration of me making out with a unicorn.

Liberals pervert language for two key reasons: to recast their side as more appealing, and to paint you as the villain. How could you be for militarization? How could you condemn something as innocent as gun control? What kind of monster would vote against a living wage? Give them a break: they're "undocumented"! What kind of chauvinism is that? Since when is an official, signed Mexican driver's license not a "document"?

You need to use their own strategy of reconfiguring

language to suit your needs—which is to shackle their destructive aims and thwart their progress.

*FOR EXAMPLE:*

* **Replace "pro-choice" with "pro-boy."** Using China as an example, being pro-choice is really "pro-boy." When couples have more control over abortive decisions, whom do they pick when it comes to gender? We already know. China is busting with young men looking for women—who aren't there. It's like an enormous English boarding school. Because they were all aborted. The next time someone says they're pro-choice, say, "Congrats, you're also 'pro-boy.'" And as science becomes even more precise about exactly what that mass of cells resting in your womb is, imagine the other "choices" you will get to make.

* **"Islamophobia" describes a reaction by many to the violence perpetrated by radical Islam.** A better term, of course, would be "psychophobia"—a fear of beheaders and other intolerant violent monsters. Radical Muslims are no different from spree killers—your fear is simply a reflection of protection of others, including like-minded, decent Muslims. In that regard, why not call yourself "pro-moderate" to describe your appreciation for Muslims who don't try to kill us? And the real bigotry is Americanophobia—as expressed by countries whose leaders shout "Death to America!" And certain world leaders who tolerate it.

* **Replace "backlash" with "coplash."** We hear "back-lash" to describe a violent reaction that rarely comes—usually after a terror attack. "Muslims fear a backlash against their community after the bombing in Boston," etc. However, we rarely are admonished against a backlash in order to protect, say, cops. No leader says, "After the Michael Brown death, it's important not to strike out at law enforcement." Often it's the opposite. Progressive politicians instead will say a singular police act represents a "deep-rooted problem." Oddly, Islamic terrorism is never ever called a "deep-rooted problem," but something detached from this religion of peace. One event in Ferguson taints an entire pro-fession; Islamic terror is erased by comparing it to the Crusades. A terrorist is just a bad apple; one bad cop represents the entire barrel. In the case of the cops, the backlash often *does* occur—as it did when a lone lunatic inspired by the relentless media coverage of the Michael Brown and Eric Garner deaths shot and killed two cops eating lunch in their patrol car. Two minority cops, by the way.

* **"Gun control."** Perhaps one of the dumbest phrases known to man, it shifts responsibility away from stop-ping criminals to stopping law-abiding citizens. Gun control has no effect on thugs; it only hinders the rest of us. It's a joke. The best way to wrest gun rights from this stupid and pointless debate is to recast it as a force equalizer for women. Gun control is actu-ally antiwoman, for it makes it harder for women to

## THE MAINSTREAM MEDIA (MSM) AND REALITY

You ever notice how the media soften the truth in the interest of tolerance?

Here's what they say, and how you recast it as fact.

**MSM:** Militants Take Revenge on Their Occupiers

**Reality:** Zealots Kill Tourists at a Bar

**MSM:** Prison Poet Publishes Book on His Personal Suffering

**Reality:** Murderer Suckers Another Lonely Editor

**MSM:** Graffiti Artist Shows Promise

**Reality:** Thug Destroys Perfectly Good Wall

**MSM:** Campus Rape at Epidemic Levels

**Reality:** Blogger Fails Statistics 101

**MSM:** Noose Found on Door Knob Seen as Hate Crime

**Reality:** Hoax Brings Attention to Troubled Soul

**MSM:** Oil Pipelines Raise Questions of Transport Safety

**Reality:** As Opposed to What? Trains? Camels?

---

**MSM:** Movie Touches on Themes of Race and Gender in Unsettling Ways

**Reality:** Movie Is Unwatchable Tripe

---

**MSM:** Radicalism Fueled by Youthful Discontent

**Reality:** He's a Fucking Terrorist

---

**MSM:** Actor Has Social Message He Wishes to Share

**Reality:** Actor Made Bank, Now Craps on Capitalism Because He Feels Self-Important

---

**MSM:** Hillary Reflects Experience of a Qualified Statesman

**Reality:** She's Entitled to This, So Give It to Her

---

**MSM:** It's a Gun-Free Zone

**Reality:** Please Shoot Us

---

protect themselves in cities like New York. No more "gun control"; call it the "gun ceiling." Say that it's time to truly reduce sexual assault by encouraging women to arm themselves. Men have 50 percent more muscle mass than women. Guns cancel that advantage out, handily. Guns make armed women and unarmed men equal. Gun control is really just "women control," and we must fight that with every fiber of our being. The best spokesman for guns is a woman. An armed, unafraid woman.

★ **Replace "e-cigarettes" with "cancerasers."** Finally, in the current fight over e-cigarettes—which are fast becoming the most effective solution in eliminating actual smoking for good—we need to make this clear: there is no such thing as an "e-cigarette." A cigarette is full of tar and other crap that kills you. If a vaping device is a cigarette, then so is a kazoo.

I'd call them cancerasers. If you replace cigarette smoking with vaping, it may be a major step toward a longer, healthier life. Right now, if you have loved ones who smoke, getting them onto vaping will mean they will be around longer than if you just let them puff away. (On the other hand, maybe that's why you want them to continue smoking.)

★ ★ ★ **11** ★ ★ ★

# CO-OPT THEIR GRIEVANCES

I've got nothing against feminists—in fact, I like to think I'm one. If feminism means a belief in equality, then I'm for that. If feminism means "girl power," then I'm for that, too. It's why I want every "girl" to own a "gun," and to "pistol-whip" me on occasion while I'm in my crushed velvet manatee onesie.

The one funny part of feminism—or at least modern feminism reflected by victims who continue to play loose with the truth and use hilarious terms like "heteronormative"—is the way in which feminists try to deny the biological reality of obvious gender differences. There's nothing more sexist than assuming one gender cannot accept scientific fact. I call this "hetero-abnormative." Or simply "silly."

**GENDER DIFFERENCES FEMINISTS DENY**

- Women are more valuable because they give birth (ew!).
- Women are more valuable because they're mothers.
- Female breasts are the perfect combination of form and function.
- Moms give better advice than your drunkest best friend.
- Grandmoms are from magical planets while grand-dads fart.
- Women remember to write thank-you notes.
- Women never destroy a bathroom.
- Women smell amazing; men smell.

The common complaint by feminists is objectification. Treating women as sex objects, solely, is pretty narrow-minded, I agree. They're great resources for making a good life, together.

But grievance must never be used as a truncheon on men. For many reasons. One: both men and women treat women like sex objects. See any cover of *Cosmopolitan,* a Victoria's Secret catalog, or a locker-room calendar (I have a collection of them, still in their original packaging). And from a biological standpoint, treating each other as sex objects was kind of the point, at least when it comes to species survival.

We've moved way beyond the savagery caused by primitive urges, but the urges still exist, and will exist forever (or until the robots take over and kill us, in around 2018 or so). Men exist, and women exist, to keep this civilization going. They pedal the procreation bike. The answer to species survival is not more senior vice presidents. If you deny that, you deny science, which feminists seem to want to do on a daily basis, because it's so "heteronormative." Apparently, a few of those heteronormals are pretty sharp, or else we wouldn't be here.

How do you combat the accusation that men treat women as mere sex objects? Heartily agree, and bemoan that the objectification does not end there. *Because as men surely treat women as sex objects, women treat men as status objects.* As P. J. O'Rourke once observed, no woman daydreams about being swept off her feet by a liberal. Bearded mixologists in Williamsburg quicken the pulse of no one, unless you're a fedora salesman.

It is a challenge—a struggle, you might say—to be a man . . . to be subjected constantly to the leering looks from women eager to see your nest-building prowess. It's true— I'm talking birds here. The attraction of status is true in birds, bees, and humans. While the male seeks markers reflective of reproductive ability, the female seeks markers of provisional prowess—the ability to protect and provide. This isn't some men's rights boilerplate shit—this is evolutionary biology accepted as fact by both scientists and drunk loud-mouths like me.

Think about how many men, young boys even, have died because of this anti-male practice. The first acrobat really was a guy trying to impress a girl. He stood on his hands and tried to walk. He fell, hit his head, and died—a casualty of female oppression through status demand. As women were objectified, men were "riskified," driven to ridiculous, idiotic deaths—causing actions in order to gain attention from women. In fact, as the old saying goes, "Men go to war so their women will watch them." So war itself is a war on men! Confused yet? So am I. But that's what happens when you take this heteronormative horsepoop to its logical conclusion.

Is it any wonder men live shorter lives than women? In order to express superior status, above and beyond our male competitors, we take risks—some noble, some idiotic. Show me a beautiful woman and it may be the last thing I see. We pull wheelies, drag race, and climb water towers. We fall off our cycles, crash our cars, and tumble to our untimely deaths. All to show females that we are made of superior stuff.

That's the real sexism. It's biological, and if you disagree with me, you must be antiscience. Probably a homophobe. Who eats left-handed, redheaded babies. Science proves that far and away the number-one cause of distress and depression in men is rejection by women. Especially hot ones. They're totally insensitive to masculine suffering. Scarlett Johansson needs to end her senseless jihad on me. I'm giving her one more year.

## Animal Rights

This grievance—that eating and/or wearing animals is cruel to the animals—is hard at first to dispute. And it's important to clarify that people who are mean to animals are in general rotten people who deserve the very worst humans have to offer (a weekend with the *HuffPo* editorial staff, or at least to be locked in a trailer with Bill Nye). However, compassion for animals is almost always a luxury that comes with wealth and leisure. There are many groups who'd eat that poor creature Paris Hilton shoves in her armpit as she boards first class (and then pick their teeth with Paris Hilton).

The anthropomorphic tendency of elitist, educated folk to think their pets are just like them misses a simple fact: almost all reciprocal love is based on survival instinct. They lick your hand, so you feed them instead of beat them. You should love them for that. But if the paw were on the other foot—they'd eat the hell out of you. Alive. (See Marie Prevost.)

## Watch-Dog Consumer List

*Which One Is Your Best Friend? The One That Whines When He Hears a Siren? Or the One That Eats Rats?*

| TRICKS FOR LIBERAL MUTTS | TRICKS FOR RIGHTWING DOGS |
| --- | --- |
| Roll over | Jump! |
| Beg | Kill! |
| Get down | Fetch! |
| Play dead | Shake. |
| Heel | Open the cooler! |

What about plants? New research shows that plants know when they're about to be victimized, and react by releasing oil-like yucky substances as a method of repelling you (I'm simplifying the science, but it pretty much sounds like what most humans do—when terrified, we crap ourselves). Everything has feelings, including that broccoli. So where does it stop? At some point we must remind everyone that the food chain is not horizontal, it's vertical. We're at the top.

That in no way means one must take advantage of such dominance. But eating an animal is not victimizing it. Since this is about grievances, one must bring up a very simple fact—that you are tired of being victimized *by* animals. When was the last time any member of the wild kingdom lifted a finger in preventing disease, in solving problems, in inventing machinery or devices that made our lives—or even theirs—easier? If you handed a monkey all the parts for a working transistor radio, he'd just eat them, and a day later poop them out from his pink ass. And the radio wouldn't even work! By this logic, it should also be okay to eat millennials, actually. But even I don't advocate that. Besides, they're pretty tasteless. Even if you brine them (not that I'd know).


Lastly, the biggest argument against animal rights will always be the argument for human rights. I cannot picket for a spotted owl while girls are kidnapped, raped, or disfigured by acid-flinging Islamists. I cannot fight for the plight of wild horses while wilder men plot the destruction of children. I cannot get worked up over Cecil the lion while

Planned Parenthood sells baby livers to the highest bidder. So while I applaud the work you do for the voiceless, remember that others are doing more important work—fighting to protect your right to spend your time in such a luxurious, self-indulgent, attention-seeking manner. Nothing is more deadly than middle-class sanctimony. Because every second spent saving the smelt is a second not devoted to annihilating ISIS. Or at least stalking Andy Cohen.

Now, if you manage to produce a cauliflower that tastes like rib eye, get back to me.

## Immigration

The pro-amnesty crowd has managed to do something simplistic but effective: paint their critics as racist. If you're against a blanket amnesty (and who carries a grudge against blankets?) and prefer an orderly solution to immigration and border control (what I quaintly call "following the law" or "establishing a country"), you must hate dark-skinned people—especially babies. Their horrible, evil, probably satanic babies.

Hardly. In fact, the amnesty crowd brazenly ignores the grievances of an already besieged minority group—young blacks. Making millions of illegal immigrants suddenly legal would likely suck away jobs that might have gone to minorities already suffering double-digit unemployment.

But then again, others say a new massive group of workers would end up using goods and services that might create new jobs. As you can see, I'm unsure myself, and starting to sweat a little. But I wouldn't mind a real debate without the accusations of bigotry.

I love immigration—and if people want to come here

and work hard, God bless them. I've even come up with a Gutfeld Homestead Act, on *The Five,* suggesting that all these new immigrants should move to dead cities like Detroit and rebuild them. Give the Mexicans Buffalo. Maybe the Bills will finally win a Super Bowl.

To be persuasively right on this, co-opt grievance. The real group victimized by amnesty? Immigrants who actually stood in line and filled out the forms. God bless 'em.

Amnesty is largely a political ploy to get votes. It's not simply harmful—it's harmful to those people who played by the rules. More important, those people who played by the rules did so because they "get" it. Meaning they "get" America, which is different from feeling they "deserve" it. People who break the law *never* feel that way—and their violations make everyone else who did the right thing the real victims.

Finally, imagine if Disneyland had no fence—if it were free to crash. Value plummets and good things become disrespected. The teacups become the pee cups and the Matterhorn becomes the Doesn't Matterhorn. You only appreciate what you earn—even Mickey Mouse knows that.

# LINK REAL LIFE TO
# FATUOUS BELIEF

As the only known conservative at my previous magazines, I worked among successful liberals. Until they talked to me, most had never realized how quickly they will abandon their liberal beliefs in their quest to be successful.

I often tangled with dedicated runners, incredibly disciplined musicians, and vicious publishers who enforce deadlines with military precision, even bosses who ruthlessly prune their herd at the first sniff of a bad sales quarter, but who were all namby-pamby leftists when they turned off all the other stuff that requires standards. You can't win a race as a liberal. You cannot win a sale as a liberal. You cannot perform an amazing version of "Dirty Deeds Done Dirt Cheap" as a liberal. All successes in life are based on conservative principles—and if these liberals applied their no-score, no-winner, no-loser belief systems to their hobbies or professions, they would fail miserably.

★ ★ ★

Success relies on absolute truths, supply and demand, work and reward, achievement, not identity. As the old saying goes, it doesn't matter if the cat is black or white, as long as it catches mice. Conservatives catch mice. Liberals apologize to them. And want you to buy them cheese so they don't have to chase mice.

It's interesting that people who participate in professions that require conservative values are often so very liberal. Here are three examples of such types, and how to expose their inner right-winger. Chances are they will never think of themselves as liberals, ever again. (Or at least they will hate you and go away.)

## Example One: The Musician

You'd think all of them are liberals, but surprisingly it's only the successful egomaniacs who can afford to be. The musicians who last the longest operate a business dependent on incredibly stringent conservative principles. If you hire a backup band, for example, they must show up on time to practice. They must be disciplined enough to understand that perfection requires attention to detail and have a basic understanding of economics to justify a grueling tour schedule (even Mick Jagger went to the London School of Economics. It's true—"Satisfaction" was about the joy of capital gains). When you go see your favorite metal band, you can bet that the whole tour is mapped out not as some hippy-dippy road trip, but as a meticulously planned endeavor to wring every penny of profit out of it. Smart musicians are often the most conservative people on the planet. Someone had to pay for the gas, the guitar strings, and the antibiotics.

## Example Two: Fitness

As a former health editor, I can attest: the government cannot give you six-pack abs (unless you get them to pay for the implants). Exercise is perhaps the best example of conservative/libertarian thinking at your disposal. For the amount of effort you put in, you reap the reward you deserve. If you pump iron for two hours, three times a week, your body will *change* as a direct result. There is nothing as concrete or as fair as this. It's the one bank where you deposit effort and you build a portfolio of reward. There is no affirmative action in exercise. One muscle doesn't get special dispensation because it's smaller or weaker. There is no minimum wage, safety net, or unemployment bennies for your glutes—you're either in shape or you're not. No one is gonna redistribute my awesome pecs. To quote Obama, "You didn't build that." Sorry, but I did.

## Example Three: Cooking

There are buttloads of cooking shows these days, populated by spiky-haired women and tattooed love-patched beardos from Brooklyn. They all look so Occupy Wall Street—but when they enter the kitchen they become the Wolves of Wall Street. There are no feelings behind that butcher block; there's no room for "if it feels good, do it." A recipe is a recipe for a reason: a dictum designed to make sure *anyone* can repeat this nutritional equation. If you can make baked Alaska with these ingredients and instructions, then so can I. Conservativism is all about following directions. Cooking is really just building a successful enterprise, with food. And it must taste good, not fulfill a greater good.

Liberals are bad cooks but great eaters.

**BEST JOBS FOR A LEFTIST**

Who needs standards if it feels good? These are dead-end jobs for dead-end brains:

- symbolic die-in coordinator (previous experience in shouting at tourists)

- concerned protester—entails facing off looming police officer during march (only young, hot females with rich parents need apply)

- euphoric anarchist (entails brick throwing, and rocking cars back and forth—ideal for male with daddy issues)

- sign manager (distributing identical placards to jobless people who are paid to hold them)

- mob extra—must look angry, but frightened, as cops approach (females preferred, but will take minorities of either gender)

- Guy Fawkes mask wearer—experience in gesticulating wildly at local news affiliate anchor (all ages welcome; ideal for professors)

Following recipes is the opposite of liberalism, where demanding excellence (that requires objective measures) is seen as hurtful.

Restaurants that require reservations weeks or months in advance got that way because of reliance on a diligent work ethic that led to a reputation for great food. You cannot reach that pinnacle without being a competitive, results-oriented asshole, in other words, a capitalist. It's a *very* tough business. Fact is, the beauty of capitalism is that it moves hand in hand with quality. *Do* something great and great things happen to you. You put in the hours in the kitchen, you make a great taco. While this seems so obvious, it's no longer so in schools. Instead our children are taught that identity is more important than industry. This may work when teaching gender studies, but not when cooking a seafood gumbo. It's why gender-studies majors can barely toast a PopTart.

### Example Four: Sports

There are no progressives in locker rooms. There are no liberals on playing fields. The goal is to score, to beat your opponents, to defeat them. Not just degrade them, but demolish them. You want to crush the adversary. That's about as conservative as you can possibly get. And about as lovey-dovey as a head on a stick. Is there a sport that is progressive in philosophy? Yes. It's called tag. Liberalism is tag in which the successful are always "it."

## BEST LIBERAL SPORTS

- tag
- musical chairs (as long as there's a chair for every player)
- unfunded mandated volleyball
- anything not for "keepsies"

★ ★ ★ **13** ★ ★ ★

# BREAK THE SCOLD MOLD

The left finds it therapeutic to scold you for the silliest things—from improper use of pronouns, to wearing the wrong shirt to work. (For more on this topic, turn on the TV.)

The left created the fine art of complaint in the 1960s and 1970s, perfected the shrill drill during their activist politics of the 1980s, and made political correctness commonplace in the 1990s. As conservatives learned to fight the rise of PC politics, some of us adopted our adversaries' gritty strategies, but also their unseemly habits. We started turning into the scolds, exploding with outrage every time a leftist said something stupid. (Again, turn on the TV.) Perhaps because we had kept our anger bottled up for so long while having to listen to the whiners of the world leak their rage all over us, it was our turn to vent. That we did. And do.

## WHAT IS THE PERSUASIVELY INCORRECT?

Not too long ago, we saw the rise of the politically correct, in which behavior that was perceived as mean-spirited in any way, shape, or form was deemed unacceptable and shamed. It was not about your actions, but about your words. It wasn't about guilt, but about perceived intent.

While there is no doubt that the advent of the politically correct helped shame authentic bigots and assholes, it overstepped in such a manner as to threaten free speech and the casual civility of a normal, well-intentioned, and engaged society.

Then came the welcome blowback: the emergence of the "politically incorrect." It's not so much a movement as a boisterous correction: a desire to champion thinking over feeling. It's a frame of mind: identifying the "politically incorrect" is saying that you aren't trafficking in identity politics, or you're not one of the thought or language police. You're calling it straight and blunt.

However, then came idiots who used that opportunity to revert to idiotic behaviors. An overcorrection. Calling someone a fat bitch isn't being politically incorrect; it's still being a dick.

What's the next step? Something I like to call being "persuasively incorrect." That means sticking to the commonsense values that progressives and academics despise, but being able to articulate them in a manner that wins converts, rather than confirmations from like-minded people.

As I write this, a rocket scientist responsible for landing a fax machine (I'm guessing) on a comet perhaps a zillion miles away had to apologize for the shirt he wore as his accomplishments unfolded. To recap:

During the live-stream of the European Space Agency's landing of a probe on a comet 300 million miles from Earth, scientist Matt Taylor happened to be wearing a shirt featuring the artwork of women in sexy poses brandishing weapons (it was all very sci-fi, not so much sexy as it was dorky). On Twitter, scolds went mad, with idle women and men accusing him of "casual misogyny" (the name of Bill Clinton's boat). He ended up changing the shirt (thankfully, not on air), but that wasn't enough for the outrage brigade, who clearly had nothing better to do than harass someone who just *chucked something onto a comet.* (Another example of the curse of being employed—you have a job that keeps you busy. Those who attack you don't have such obstacles.)

The poor guy ended up apologizing—in tears. It was painful to watch, unless of course you're an unemployed blogger and get off on this sort of thing. You'd think when someone puts in enough effort to become a rocket scientist, he should get to wear any shirt he wants (as long as it's not Ed Hardy). Sure, the guy knew he was going to be on camera and probably could have picked something else—but he's a rocket scientist—not a fashionista. He dresses badly *because* he's a supersmart scientist who devotes his life to solving life's riddles, not trying to find leather chaps at Barneys (second floor, near the dressing room).

The fact that sad feminists on Twitter focused on his

clothing and not his achievements made them more sexist than Archie Bunker watching female wrestling.

Worse, the fact that this fellow accomplished the unfathomable, and the next moment was crying over his shirt because of Twitter, tells you how this scold scourge has turned that online world into a bully chamber. In one universe, a man achieves greatness that no other has, and in another, the Twitterverse—a petty grotesque flattening ball of hell—he is stripped of his manliness, humiliated in front of the world. The fact that he didn't tell them all to go fuck themselves shows you how removed he is from our current cultural B.S. This guy actually thought he had done something wrong.

Was the shirt sexist? Hell no. It was tacky. Awful. Garish. Grotesque, even. It was adolescent (and sort of great, really). It only showed the world a man who needed help buying clothes. It revealed that scientists are not metrosexuals (thank God), because their priorities are different. And by different, I mean "better." He'd rather figure out space than socks. But feminists got their scalp—a weeping man—and amazing progress took a backseat to a pathetic charade of "social justice." Seriously, why send a rocket to a comet if this is what you get for it? The world doesn't deserve scientists. All it deserves are assholes on Twitter who wallow in 140 characters to make up for lacking their own (character, that is, not assholes).

During this same week, by the way, conservatives were doing some scolding of their own. For Veterans Day, a concert was held in Washington, DC, and Bruce Springsteen performed the Creedence Clearwater classic "Fortunate Son."

Just as there are hacks on the left ripe to blow any outrage whistle, we have scolds, too, and they jumped on this one, claiming that Springsteen had insulted the troops with his "antimilitary" song choice.

Cable show opinion-flippers bellowed about his insulting the men who defend our country—without ever actually understanding that the song might be about people rich enough to evade the draft, not those who evaded fighting a war. It didn't matter: it just felt good to scold a celebrity! Never mind the fact that everyone enjoyed the song—including the troops.

But the scolds still scolded. Cool. Whatever. But you're really helping no one, especially yourself. I speak as a guilty party.

## FOUR REASONS WHY YOU DON'T SCOLD

- You're an adult with other stuff to do.
- Whoever you're scolding doesn't care.
- You expend your energy on garbage that dissipates in forty-eight hours.
- By scolding, you become a scold. Which is somebody nobody likes. You just succeed in turning conservatives into the town elders in *Footloose*.

Scolding is nitpicking, by definition. Springsteen didn't hurt anyone. He didn't steal anything. He didn't encourage violent revolution or bully a scientist over a lousy shirt. He performed, and if his song choice bugs you, swallow the bug and move on. Or—here's a revelation—change the channel!

"But it pisses me off, Greg. That song was a slap in the face to my dad, who served!"

Okay, hypothetical guy—if it does upset you, how do you respond to it without falling into the trap of manufactured stridency, where the condemnation of a pop star over a song is on par with the emotion you might normally reserve for ISIS? How do you expose a legitimate error without coming off like a TV screamer trying to cash in on easy emotion? (The first way to do this: don't go on TV. I have enough competition.)

If Springsteen really bugs you, if Lena Dunham really bugs you, if Bill Maher really bugs you, then pursue their perspective to its absurd conclusion. Absurdity *always* ends up servicing your point better (at least among the intelligent) than if you were to voice sincere, even appropriate anger.

Example: Recently a woman panhandler was seen leaving her normal spot where she begs for change, in a Mercedes-Benz. Apparently this woman hangs out at a San Diego shopping mall, sometimes with a dude, begging for cash—and is seen, according to one report, driving "off laughing in a Mercedes-Benz." Sounds suspiciously like Nancy Pelosi, but anyway.

This is fodder for reflexive outrage—an indictment of the lazy freeloader who pretends to be down on her luck but really isn't. So rather than condemn . . . do the opposite: applaud. She should serve as an inspirational model for other panhandlers. By begging, and driving off in a Mercedes, she's saying to others, "See, if you work hard enough at panhandling, one day you can have all this, too!" In fact, we should set up a federal job training program for people who beg for money. (Oh, that's right, we have one already—it's called "public television." My mistake.) Most people appreciate a break from the predictable rage.

## Why Are Liberals Angry About This ... and Not That?

| THIS | THAT |
|---|---|
| incorrect pronouns for the transgendered | gays flung from rooftops |
| not enough gender-neutral bathrooms | women's hands chopped off for cellphone use |
| Barbie dolls creating unrealistic body types | women beaten for driving |
| men clumsily flirting at work | twelve-year-old girls forced to marry |

There. You make your point, and you make it without sounding like a dickhead. That's the point of this book, really. ("Making Your Point, Without Being a Dickhead"—a title my narrow-minded publisher rejected, by the way.)

A final point on scolding: as a conservative, you will always have the disadvantage in the outrage wars. Kyle Smith said as much in the *New York Post* last November: when a Republican opens himself to attack, it doesn't matter if the flaw has little or no impact on policy. Still, the outrage bell rings loud and long. But if a liberal is exposed for lying—or rather actually confesses deception—it's explained away, even if the corrupt act had a massive impact on the American population ("If you like your doctor, you can keep . . ."). You have a complicit media playing silent, because in this bank robbery they drove the getaway car. And they willingly excuse a lie for the greater good, even when the greater good kills. Sometimes that's the point.

The media, however, sees it in reverse—salivating over the right's marginal transgressions, avoiding huge malfeasance on the left. It's something we have to adjust for, which means letting go of problem candidates who can't stop saying dumb stuff. And we have them. Does a belief in limited government and states' rights somehow cause Tourette's? Because we have candidates saying more dumb shit than Ted Turner and Mel Gibson on a three-day bender. Together. In Vegas. With Michael Richards driving.

### POLITICAL TOURETTE'S

Red meat you can avoid saying, because everyone else already says it too many times:

* phrases like "Obummer"

* blaming the "lame stream media"—just call them assholes

* bringing up impeachment every time Obama farts

* suggesting Obama is a Muslim because he might be one

* George Soros is behind everything (although, he is)

## ★ ★ ★ 14 ★ ★ ★

# EMBRACE THE INNER SKEPTIC

99.9 percent of everything said in the media comes without proof.

Including, of course, that statement. My head hurts.

But it's true. Think about most of the opinions—or rather *all* of the opinions—you hear every day.

> *"I stopped drinking Diet Coke because it makes you fat."*
> *"Fracking makes your tap water catch on fire."*
> *"During the Super Bowl, men beat up their women more than usual, because of sports and stuff."*

Almost all the stuff you're told, especially health-wise, anyway, is bullshit. Because real health information requires actual research, which takes decades—and sucks. I don't know anyone who's died from drinking Diet Coke, but there are plenty of doctors who gave themselves heart attacks trying to get published in *The New England Journal of Medicine.*

I'm told by too many of my educated friends that Diet Coke is bad for me, and I should stop drinking it. "Diet Coke is bad for you," a pal will say, without bothering to look at oncoming traffic as he crosses Ninth Avenue.

Seriously, how many people have been hit by cars or buses because they were busy scrolling down their iPhone looking for a story on gluten allergies? (Answer: 15,000 every year, per the Gutfeld Institute of Mind Blowing Facts.)

I have no proof (who needs it), but I maintain that more people die from horrible accidents while screeching into their phones about health scares than die in the actual health scares themselves. Every month a person gets run over by a dump truck just as they were yakking away about Ebola going airborne. Instead, *they* went airborne.

The natural state for your intellect must be at rest—kicking back in the beanbag chair I call skepticism. Skepticism must be your guide, or else you will be lost. You will believe anything, and bounce through life like a skittish pinball, flipped from one hysteria to the next, on edge that something, somewhere is going to kill you. Meanwhile what really gets you is what you never see coming (see the dump truck, above).

Skepticism, however, must not be confused with psychosis. While it's important to be wary of things portrayed in the media and by opportunistic politicians, it is important not to afford legitimacy to the unbalanced who deny actual events we've seen with our own eyes. People confuse skeptics with conspiracy aficionados—but the latter are usually the most gullible people on earth.

Truthers about 9/11 are not skeptics—they are narcissists who use tragic events to play a game of "I know something you don't." It's the adult equivalent of that obnoxious third-grade classmate telling you, "Oh, I know a secret!" just to infuriate you. They claim to question a set of obvious facts with spurious reasoning, and then insist that the burden is on you to disprove their idiocy. This is not skepticism. This is time-wasting twaddle, perfected by tools desperate for attention. Do not waste your time with such rabble, and realize that denial of facts doesn't constitute skepticism. Skepticism denies nothing, but questions unsubstantiated opinion and, more than ever, hypothetical models that tell you the earth is burning up. So how does one employ skepticism wisely, in a manner that helps you find the truth, while explaining to others where they may have gone wrong? By picking the right targets.

### THINGS YOU SHOULD BE SKEPTICAL OF, AT ALL TIMES

* **Any media that seems overly invested in an idea.** As a rule, something that creates disciples in the media is never what it turns out to be, whether it concerns climate change models, gun control, or the "natural beauty" of Kim Kardashian's ass.

* **Self-imposed spokesmen of any kind who seem feverishly strident and humorless in the zeal for their cause.** You see this in cults, in truthers, and in college classes. Once someone stakes out a controversial or dramatic point of view, they real-

ize they are rewarded by spotlights, guest segments, and—if they're lucky—a book contract. Al Sharpton made a TV career riding dual horses called hysteria and hoaxes. The guy actually got rich and powerful (and invited to the White House) off a lie about a girl covered in feces. Only trust those who have nothing to gain. Which eliminates everyone.

* **Any sweeping language.** When a person throws words around like "unanimous" or "overwhelming," it clues you in that they don't want you to press too hard for their facts. I am willing to debate you on gun control, but I always allow myself the possibility that I might be proven wrong. That makes me (theoretically) pleasant to be around, and also right most of the time, because I prepare to be wrong. In the arena of climate change, we hear about this unanimous group of scientists—the 97 percent, and so on. Once you look closer, it's way less certain about anything. Real scientists and engineers traffic in certainty when they're working with scientific laws that make the world work. But they do not magically pretend to know what happens next . . . unless of course there is grant money involved.

* **A definitive finding.** Science is the act of clawing our way to some semblance of knowledge . . . a truth that will become less truthful or more truthful the more you claw. Every day I figure out something about life that I didn't know before. It blows my mind, until the next day, when I uncover something else that makes that certainty slightly less certain. (For instance, yesterday

I was sure Spider-Man could beat Daredevil. Today I'm racked with doubt.) There are obvious truths: when you see a plane hit a building, and that building falls— the only people questioning that are assholes.

**A WALLET-SIZED LIST OF ASSHOLES***

Mark Ruffalo
Woody Harrelson
Martin Sheen
Charlie Sheen (runs in the family)
Ed Asner
Rosie O'Donnell
Janeane Garofalo

---

*9/11 truthers

★ In any instance in which you're asked to suspend your skepticism, those cases are always man-made. Meaning, whether it be a political movement or an ideological crusade or an assertion that Kanye West is a "genius"—they only reject your skepticism if in fact the phenomenon was created by a man, or a group of men. You can't be skeptical about a tree, an earthquake, or a kitten. But register skepticism about a movement and you wind up dead. This is why climate change has surpassed most cults in devotional zeal. Point out that the man-made predictions have not accurately translated into biological realities, and you are not deemed wrong, you are deemed a heretic. The comical notion that you're a flat-earther makes no sense—since it was "established science" that clung to such beliefs. Remember, at one point *every* scientist was a flat-earther, because everyone, every single person, thought the world was flat (this was disproved around 1986, I believe). When a few people finally raised their hands and said, "Nope, round," they got burned at the stake. By scientists.

**SKEPTIC OR JUST CRAZY?**

Which of these thoughts have crossed your mind?

A. Chemtrails. Can I send you an email on Chemtrails?

B. Bill Nye the Science Guy seems a bit messed in the head.

C. Vaccines—do you really know what's in them?

D. How did that building come down, seriously?

E. You think Hillary will sign my photo of Vince Foster?

F. The birth certificate . . . the birth certificate!

G. I can't believe that it's not butter.

H. I've never seen bin Laden and Dana Perino in the same room.

(crazy: A, C, D, E, F; skeptic: B, G, H )

★ ★ ★ **15** ★ ★ ★

# LOOK LIKE THEM

You know what depresses me? If I can turn the sound off on a TV and still be able to tell if the person on-screen is a Republican. The stereotype of an older white male exists because it's true. Sometimes we have women, too. Today, on TV, I saw one white, southern, female, religious, conservative talking head say she was refusing to see *Fifty Shades of Grey* because it was a threat to marriage. Her outrage couldn't have been scripted better by *The Onion*. The casting agency nailed it. I felt sad (so I ate a chicken smothered in peanut butter).

My point: sometimes you should just admit the opposition has something on you, and then work like a mad dog to fix it.

We need diversity, not for diversity's sake, but because it actually helps the country. It makes the nation a better place.

Also, it's fun. After all—think about what the left is most terrified of.

Think about what drives them batshit crazy.

It's not a guy who looks like Orrin Hatch. Or a woman who looks like Phyllis Schlafly. It's a guy who looks like Tim Scott, and a woman who looks like Mia Love. Nothing upsets a liberal more than someone who is *supposed* to be liberal—a black, Hispanic, or gay conservative. I've seen it happen. Bring up a conservative black leader (like, say, Allen West) and you see steam pour out from the lefty's head—like a malfunctioning robot in a low-budget sci-fi movie. "Does not compute! Does not compute!" they mechanically wail, as their stiff arms desperately flail for something to steady their shocked system. It also reveals their secret bigotry—assuming blacks must adhere to specific beliefs. Only an infusion of craft beer and kale will help them recover.

A black right-winger is kryptonite to a white elitist liberal. When an "afri-con" enters the room, white liberals forget to check their privilege, and instinctively decide that they know better. They shut down. And then they lose. Which is why Mia Love won. I mean, a black, female Mormon. That staccato popping sound you hear is the collective synapses of the *New York Times* editorial board frizzing out. As I write this, washed-up actor George Takei just called Clarence Thomas "a clown in black face." Then offered a piss-poor nonapology.

Black liberals love to call black conservatives "house negroes" (or variations on that N-word). White liberals are actually worse: they simply hate conservative blacks. Even those who are true heroes. Ben Carson has saved more children's lives than all the members of the Congressional Black

Caucus combined, which makes his gaffes forgivable. He was too busy saving babies to keep up on changing times.

The reason for left-wing antipathy toward conservatives who aren't white is twofold: they can't label them racist or homophobic, and one more gay or black for us is one less gay or black for them. And God forbid it becomes a trend! It threatens the existence of their strip mall of collective identity blocs.

Which is why, for the Republican Party to grow and succeed in places where it hasn't before, it needs to do the most shallow (but perhaps most important) thing: look like the left.

That's all. Look like them.

It's not enough to be the party of red white and blue. It has to be the party of black, brown, pink, yellow, and purple. And mauve. Why not?

Try this the next time when you're in a debate, in conversation, or trying to make a point at a bar: quote people who look like Democrats. The Allen Wests, the Susan Martinezes, the Stefanicks and Rubios. Instead of saying, "Well, Glenn Beck says that unicorns are the Antichrist," say, "Mia Love has spoken eloquently on satanic unicorns. What, you don't know who Mia Love is? Let me show you. . . ." Trust me. You will suddenly be regarded as a genius.

And what about new arrivals—illegal immigrants now staying thanks to Obama's amnesty? Do we write them off, or do we sell our philosophical goods to them? You know my answer:

Every immigrant is an ally.

Immigrants are almost always naturally conservative (see Arnold Schwarzenegger—just not in a Speedo). Most come here to succeed, to build a life—not to live off some-one else. Many escape countries where the government is their total safety net but also their mortal enemy. Which is why they come here to risk everything (including their lives). I mean, this country produced Skrillex, Kathy Griffin, and yoga pants. And people *still* come here. You know they must want it, bad.

We need to get these people on our side, and stop assuming they're gimmes for lazy leftists. It's hard for me to fathom that a family-oriented religious Mexican believes what your typical prog academic spews. They have more in common with Limbaugh than with the left. I can't believe for a second that a young Cuban actually looks at an Occupy Wall Streeter and thinks, "I want to be like that. I want to crap in the street and eat out of garbage cans." No, he thinks, "Christ, I just *left* that."

## What Diversity Looks Like

| RIGHTWING | LEFTWING |
| --- | --- |
| Ben Carson | Ben Affleck |
| Mia Love | Mia Farrow |
| Thomas Sowell | Tom Steyer |
| Al West | Al Gore |
| Texas | Gwyneth Paltrow |
| Tim Scott | George Clooney |
| Stacey Dash | Rosie O'Donnell |

★ ★ ★

There is a challenge, however: where these immigrants came from is often a place so much worse than where they end up in America.

Their expectations are way different from yours—which presents a problem for Republicans who wish to preach aspirational values that run counter to the left. Immigrants understand opportunity and money and comfort and warmth—but they're not going to be won over by the privatization of Social Security, or battles over the death tax. You need to recruit, and to speak their language—which is often the language you speak to yourself.

If I were a superrich conservative, I'd create a program called the "American People Who Work for Food and Stock Options" ("APWWFSO")—a new, free class that explains what makes this country a success, teasing out the equation that enticed immigrants to flee here in the first place:

**ASSIMILATION + HARD WORK − ENTITLEMENT ×
LONG-TERM OPTIMISM FOR FUTURE GENERATIONS + INTACT
FAMILY STRUCTURE × COMMUNITY INTERACTION = SUCCESS**

(Koch brothers, give me a call—we'll talk.)

Perhaps the APWWFSO—a reform movement focused on an appreciation of the basic principles, values, and history of the greatest country ever—could be free but tied to employment. It could be something that companies strongly encourage new arrivals applying for work to attend. I've already got the motto: "You take this class, we'll hire your ass." Wouldn't that look great on a flag flying proudly over US immigration headquarters? I've even sketched the mascot, and yes, it's naked and has a horn. Which I admit is, like, so last Saturday night. But it never gets old.

145

★ ★ ★ **16** ★ ★ ★

# STOP EATING YOUR MODERATES

The key to all politics, besides having great hair, influential friends in high places, and attractive children who don't mutilate animals, is to avoid the extreme. There's no benefit from indulging the rabidly partisan. We call these people ideologues. I call them annoying. These are the people who often say, "I used to like you, until you disagreed with me on blah-blah-blah." There are tons on the left, but there's no shortage on the right. And they cost us elections. Ideology is the enemy of truth, someone famous once said (it might have been Yoda).

If you think someone is too far on the fringe, chances are he is. This is not to say, "Move to the middle." No, this is to say, "Win, for God's sake." And winning is getting all your friends together in a room with a keg of beer, and voting for a winner. It's not eating someone alive because they disagree with you on 5 percent of the issues.

## THE BEST WINNING TEAM

Politics is like *The Dirty Dozen:* a bunch of like-minded people who happen to be unlike each other—but together create a formidable force. We can all win, if we stop trying to call one another losers. Here's the recipe for disaster: ideologues calling everyone else "squishies" or "rhinos." And nonideologues returning the favor by calling them nuts.

A recipe for winning: a group that works together. A group like this:

- the wacky but intensely well-read libertarian who loves guns and Snowden

- the substantive foreign policy adult who knows defense, understands our enemies, and would strangle Snowden with a shoelace

- the paleoconservative who hates modern life but bites the bullet around gay marriage and pot proponents

- the establishment Republican who wins elections and has no time for ideology. Owns thirty-three pairs of identical khakis, and two blue blazers.

- the smart messenger who keeps everyone from fucking up on comments about social issues

- the conservative who despises any moralism from his own side

- the black lesbian veteran

Republicans losing elections is bad for the country—but it's great for people like me, and for the media in general. We still get to show up for work and scream. Which is why so many of my peers edge to the extreme: it gets them attention, which seems like success. But it isn't.

The country contains 317 million people (if you count Portland). Those are the people you want. Even if every single fan of Michael Savage votes, the Democrats still win. You need conversions, not confirmations.

Everyone is guilty at one time or another of "teamism," of going to the extreme because it's mistakenly perceived as being truer to the cause than those who are less aggro. It's actually not. The quieter guy is playing chess. The screamer is playing tic-tac-Doh. Ultimately they always screw up. (And I'm playing Chutes and Ladders. It's therapeutic.)

Look at it from a sports perspective. If we are all on the same team, playing hard is great. But while picking fights or ball hogging gets you eyeballs, it scores no points. All it gets is a wedgie in the locker room.

Play to win, not for retweets.

Ideologues repeatedly remind us that if we indulge them, we do not deserve to win. To avoid this, remember these two invaluable tips:

## Don't Pick the Wrong Battles

There are many fights out there—in fact, the wars are so numerous, you could make a living off them (burp). But the only dude who is required to engage on every issue is the fella like me who broadcasts every day. We have a massive bucket to fill, which calls for having an opinion

## HOW RIGHT-WING ARE YOU?

The "I'm more conservative than you" game leads you to make two key mistakes. You pick ridiculous battles, and you overshoot in battles you can win. You take a winning recipe and sprinkle bitter salt all over it.

How dangerous is it to box people? Here are qualities that measure your own ideology. Rate each one, 1 to 10, to see where you lie! Or lay (not sure)!

_____ "Loves limited government"

_____ "Loves limited government but hates coarse language"

_____ "Thinks public safety bows before private freedom"

_____ "Thinks spying enables freedom through security"

_____ "Thinks America should lead"

_____ "America should stay out of everything"

_____ "Vaccines are a government conspiracy"

_____ "Hates restrictions on roller coasters"

_____ "Snowden is a hero"

_____ "Seat belts and stop signs limit my rights as an individual"

_____ "I should be able to have sex with a wombat"

**Scoring:** _70–80: Rand Paul. 80 or above: Ru Paul._
_100-plus: Minneapolis–St. Paul._

on every single thing that matters, and every single thing that doesn't. It's not just politics or war. Every three days or so, I have to think of something to say about junk like the royal family or some Hollywood star's "awareness-raising" campaign—which is like trying to take a crap when all you've eaten in weeks is glue.

This doesn't mean you should follow that example. I am paid to pontificate—and we do it to entertain, not always to win.

When two major conservative icons choose, within days, to defend Bill Cosby over the onslaught of rape allegations, you gotta ask . . . why? Sure, it could be construed as brave, and perhaps refreshing ("oh look, they're going against the grain"). But please, when there are fifteen-plus (at the time) allegations of sexual abuse? By failing to consider how you defending a serious cad makes conservatism look (since you are symbolic of the movement), you drag the movement back into the whole "war on women" bullshit. It's the right-wing equivalent of Ed Asner defending Mumia Abu-Jamal, the cop killer. It becomes a magnet for your critics to expose weird, wacky extremism. Pick your battles, folks. Seriously, there is so much going on. Do you really need to defend every creep? You only have so much time on this planet.

## Don't Put Fritos on Pizza

When libs screw up—whether it's blaming a terrorist act on a video, or boasting about lying to a stupid public about

Obamacare—we often follow up with our own screwup. We see Benghazi and Jonathan Gruber as outrages, but instead of persuasively damning those who are guilty, we sloppily pile on other idiocies. In effect, we put Fritos on a pizza, when all we needed to do was serve the pizza.

Take Benghazi. In November 2014, a two-year investigation by the House Intelligence Committee (run by Republicans!) found no impropriety in responding to the 2012 attack on our compound in Libya.

But here's the key point: the White House incorrectly asserted that the terror attack was the spontaneous outgrowth of a protest over an anti-Muslim video made by some dude in America. Did Susan Rice or President Obama intentionally blame a movie to keep the blame off their policies, to help save O's re-election? To me, that's the big question—and it's really the only question that matters. And it pointed to only two possible explanations:

1. Obama is like the Obamacare architect Jonathan Gruber—he thought Americans were so stupid that they'd believe anything about the health-care bill. It's the same with saying that an Islamic terror attack on 9/11 was about a video, not about a crazed version of Islam and an insufficient security apparatus.

2. Obama truly believed radical Islamists weren't at fault and that a video was truly to blame. If that's the case, then we may have the most naive president in history, or the most dangerous one in history. To somehow explain away an attack on an obscure, mean-spirited video is something only a grad stu-

dent with a grudge would do. To witness an act of physical evil and blame it on words, or art, is pretty frightening. It's still mind-boggling that we put the director behind bars over a film, and yeah, I get it, he's kind of a tool—but the very idea is appalling. If this country was about locking people up for horrible films, Oliver Stone would be doing life. And if you believe this decision was correct, then be consistent and arrest the director of *The Interview* as well. Send Seth Rogen to Gitmo! (In fact, let's send him there whether you believe it or not.)

The conclusion from the Benghazi mess points to a moral and philosophical failing of an administration obsessed with blaming the West first (and last). The question "who pushed the video?" was the only question that should have been pursued in this inquiry. Which is why the White House was relieved when the right started to pile on assorted other conspiracies—because it made the whole investigation appear absurd. No matter how deep your antipathy might be for President Obama, to assert he was happy to let Americans die in Libya comes off as batty.

## HOW HILLARY EXPLAINED BENGHAZI

1. Guy turns on YouTube because he wants to see adorable cat videos.

2. Sees a different video about Muhammad.

3. Instead of his normal piano lessons, or dance class, he gets enraged.

4. Calls his friends to meet up (they're all free, as it turns out!).

5. Plan of action: burn down a consulate—and surprisingly, all his casual buddies are totally on board with it! What are the odds of that? On 9/11?

6. They burn down a consulate, murder everyone—and it was all on an angry whim. Not a single person stops to think it was "a little much." They were in the moment!

7. Apparently these happenstance rioters return to their normal lives as salesmen, accountants, and gardeners.

Watching the hearings, I hoped that one single Republican might articulate why the misjudgment on the video was so damn important. Perhaps I missed it. (I might've nodded off. C-SPAN is not the same without James Traficant.)

I get the other issues: Why couldn't we protect our guys? Why couldn't we get there in time? But these are not questions of moral corruption, but illustrations of insufficient support, of incompetence. Governments ARE incompetent. As Republicans we *know* that already. The government was not prepared. Because Obama didn't have troops nearby to begin with, our forces were too far away to intervene.

The "who pushed the video" question is a different matter, for it's about an *ideology* that contributes to injury. When people attack us, normally we blame the attackers—not some video the attackers might have caught on Netflix. This was a first. Conceivably, why not blame the World Trade Center attacks on *Tootsie*?

This is Obama's gaping flaw. Every terrorist act is either random workplace violence or the fault of insensitive filmmaking. He's not a president at this point; he's a guidance counselor covering for a favorite student.

Sadly (and predictably) for the right, they got greedy, laying blame on the president for the murders, when they could have simply explained the immorality of the "video defense." They should have kept it simple.

Yes, keep it simple. *Argue within your ability to explain, and your listeners' ability to understand.*

### HOW TO EXPOSE INJUSTICE

1. *Exercise self-control.* If you find the wrongdoing, focus on it, instead of spreading it around. Avoid listening to the conspiracy junkies. The moral failing of blaming a video is more than enough to hang your anger on.

2. *Mock mercilessly.* How do you blame terror on a video? Would you blame rape on the victim's clothing? Isn't that what Islamophobia is? Our embassy

workers died because a video enticed such rage? The Benghazi video is the Democratic Party's equivalent of going out at night without a bra.

3. *Avoid political mantras.* Do not repeat "Benghazi" whenever you feel it's appropriate. Benghazi is not just a tragedy, it's a symptom of a more disturbing behavior: a president who denies external evil because he's obsessed with the sins of his own country, which he intended to fix. The enemy cannot be wrong if he already assumes we're the guilty party.

## ★ ★ ★ **17** ★ ★ ★

# OMBUDSING YOUR BUDDIES

When some famous lefty says something stupid, I laugh (which means I laugh a lot at the Pope). And then I inevitably grouse that the media completely ignores the gaffe. When someone on the right pulls a bone-headed move, I die a little inside, knowing it will reflect badly on all of us. When a right-winger makes a crude joke, reports of it are tacked up on trees in Papua New Guinea. If I had tweeted what Trevor Noah had tweeted about Jews, I'd be tossed into the ocean from a helicopter.

This chapter isn't to complain that one side gets more grief than the other over gaffes. We already know that. The right always has a target on its back; the left's back is sore from all the patting. Which means the right's behavior has to always be superior to the left's. If more of us don't infiltrate the media and/or pop culture, then really, we need to be damn close to perfect. So stop whining, and change.

When *Red Eye* started, I had a problem with Andy Levy, a potential cast member. He was a very intelligent guy—thoughtful, funny, and libertarian. But in the "I can shout louder than you can" world of cable TV, there was no place for him. In a medium that demands sprinkles on its ice cream, he was sand.

Thankfully for the show (and for Andy) we came up with the "in-show ombudsman." This idea was initially meant to make sure Andy had a job (he owed me money), but it also made sense, because Andy was born to play the job: an emotionless, fact-based robot with steel-blue eyes, whose only mission was to correct your errors—never to compliment your emotional palaver. He would be the island of logic in a sea of raging hysterics.

For the first four years of *Red Eye,* Andy appeared in the middle of the show to correct falsehoods, exaggerations, and other nonsense spouted by conservative guests, liberal guests, and me (especially me).

His segment was wildly popular among fans. But our fear was that people were going to bed after thinking the show was over. So we scuttled it and put Andy on the table as a permanent panelist. (Yeah, it took us four years. I only realized it was an issue when I noticed the crew had left after Andy's segment.)

The lesson from the *Red Eye* ombudsing experiment? *While it's easy to critique your adversaries, it's more important to correct your allies.* Because their mistakes, left to fester, will come back to haunt you. Every conservative should have an ombudsman, if only to sharpen their skills so they can go out and beat the crap out of their opponents (especially if you're a conservative in public life). Ombudsing prevents you from repeating the same mistakes—or worse, reporting crap that people send you in emails. Facing a critic each and every day allows you the chance to rethink your own blinkered assumptions. Every conservative needs an Andy Levy. It's why I couldn't even let my pal, Donald Trump, off the hook for his jab at John McCain.

More important, it makes your point of view more attractive, because you are shown to be brave enough to withstand criticism, and do so publicly. In my opinion, the weakest people in the room are those who embrace lockstep—from the left or right. They weaken any cause and undermine its aims—for they refuse to test the strength of their own beliefs.

## Example One: Panic

During the Ebola scare of 2014, conservatives wigged out. Those who rely on facts to discuss guns and climate change seemed to abandon that calm sobriety to the "we're all gonna die" mantra that was born not from science but from a mistrust of the government.

The mistrust is thoroughly understandable (after a year of scandals largely ignored by the media, it seemed the White House could get away with anything, including, to some, allowing a disease to ravage a country). But that notion was harmful, and wrong. If you're a conservative and you want to be taken seriously, you need to stick to the facts, even if that helps the guy you disagree with, currently in the White House. During the Ebola crisis, we witnessed idiotic conspiracy theories erupting on every network. I saw my job as a "nutjob fireman." Meaning whenever someone said something crazy about the disease (It's airborne! Obama wanted it to come here!), I would show up with my fire hose of logic and put the idiot fire out.

## Example Two: Snowden

A lot of people on the right called him a hero. The fact is, many of his fans on the right would not have been his fans if his leaks had been done under a Republican. Then he would have been shot. I said as much—ombudsing the ideological reflex of my cohorts—for I believe that Snowden compromised our nation's security. Some evidence suggests ISIS altered its behavior based on information culled from the Snowden/Greenwald leaks. Further, literally every member of America's national security apparatus whom I've seen questioned on this contends that Snowden's damage to us is incalculable. And one must wonder why Snowden went to Glenn Greenwald, a character who blamed the October 2014 terror attack in Canada, on Canada. Greenwald is a man with more than a hobbyist's interest in anti-Western ideology, and a mocking hatred for the war on terror. The right made a mistake embracing this man Snowden, who as I write is holed up in Moscow with his Oscar statue. Funny how that all worked out. If you don't think he's working for Russia, then you don't know Russia. Putin has the guy in an invisible cage. (Maybe we can do an Oscar-worthy exchange? Let's offer Steven Segal.) The right's embrace of Snowden gave Obama and liberals an edge in the adult arena of espionage, terror, and security.

Speaking of movies: I wonder if all those in Hollywood who branded this man a hero felt the same way after all their info was leaked in the Sony affair? Leaking national security information is heroic, but leaking your jokes about Obama is not?

Look: If we are going to be consistent about our nation's security, then that means you support the NSA under Obama, the same way you did under Bush. Anything else makes you a hypocrite. If you wish to be taken seriously, divorce your team loyalties from an issue before you make your position known. Who knows. As much as it hurts, you and Obama might be on the same page. Trust me, it will last only a minute.

## Example Three: Elections

If you don't ombuds the candidates favored by your easily excitable, like-minded ideologues, you end up losing elections. You end up with Christine O'Donnell—a nice enough person who might have been a witch, but cost the Republicans a Senate seat.

Backed by the Tea Party (which I've lauded), she defeated Michael Castle in the 2010 Republican primary in Delaware for the US Senate. Castle was a better candidate, a nine-term US representative, and he probably would have had a better chance of beating Chris Coons. We'll never know because O'Donnell beat Castle, and then got trounced by Coons by a margin of 57 to 40 percent. Essentially, we brought a broomstick to a gunfight.

Why did O'Donnell get the nod over Castle in the first place? She was a lightweight, spending much of her time running for office, even as a write-in. She got as far as she did because we (I include myself) refused to ombuds her. Bored by the typical narrative of most political races, we saw her as a fun antidote to the Republican establishment, a simplistic notion that satisfied emotional urges to purge—to go for purity over practicality. It wasn't smart. It was the equivalent of an unsatisfying one-night stand for a happily married guy (I don't know this from experience).

I remember when she was making the talk-show rounds, you could sense she was not the real deal. When I met her, I didn't sense a candidate, but a reality show contestant.

We would have done better with Triumph the Insult Comic Dog. (He's better on trade policy.)

Ombudsing separates the amateurs from the pros. It forces you to step up your game and cuts the tether to toxic ideology: the kind of thing that forces you to make stupid choices for the sake of the "team." We all want to be team players. But let's not be the '62 Mets. The winning team is pro-win, not pro-litmus.

It's better to critique yourself before you walk out into the real world and get nailed by those who really want to see you fail. The ombudsman is the voice in your head that reminds you of the bigger picture. It tells you to enjoy the distractions but quickly discard them. It tells you that winners don't follow Twitter trends. A winner must be hard on himself before others get their shot. And as a conservative, you can bet they will always get their shot.

# 18

# HOW TO BE RIGHT

## USING METAPHORS, SIMILES, AND OTHER CRAP

Sometimes the only way to make a persuasive argument about something is to compare it to something else. For example: buying this book for a friend is like donating a kidney to a stranger—an exercise in heroic selflessness (so buy three).

Metaphors and similes are excellent weapons in the war against nonsense. In short, a metaphor is a figure of speech using one thing to mean another. "Men are pigs" is a good start.That metaphor becomes a simile when you add "like." "Men are like pigs." So a metaphor "is" and a simile is "like." As for analogies, that's the logical culmination of what you've expressed using a mountain of metaphors. Thank you, Mrs. Brady (sixth-grade writing class, during which I mostly pondered Melissa Parms's legs as the new mystery of the universe).

**DIY METAPHOR KIT**

Instructions: Match something from the left column with something from the right, then amuse your friends by saying the resulting metaphor right out loud!
    Match 'em up and put "is" in the middle!

| | |
|---|---|
| Al Gore | a dock covered in dead tuna |
| Tom Steyer | a bucket of dead bait |
| Bernie Sanders | circus livestock |
| Al Sharpton | a weenie |

Metaphors: they're a crutch—and they feel good when they work. And who doesn't like a crutch that makes you feel good? (I dated one for six months.) When you find the right metaphor to explain exactly what you want to explain, it produces immense relief, like releasing your belt after a disgusting meal (or removing your pants on an airplane).

Of course, if they're too complicated, or wordy, then you lose the impact. A metaphor is designed to simplify a complicated idea so the recipient's brain goes "aah" when it digests your comparison.

Here are examples of my more successful ones (I keep a low bar on this).

*"If America were a house, the left would root for the termites."*
This illustrates the innate desire of the left to em-

brace any cause that undermines the foundations of the country. They are termites.

Referring to the Bowe Bergdahl swap:
*"President Obama just traded five cruise missiles for a squirt gun."*

*"The media is Obama's scandal condom."*
Let's explain that one: the media has operated for the last six to seven years as a bubble that insulates the president from the effects of his own risky, indulgent behavior. Whether it's the Justice Department scandal, the VA mess, the Obamacare deceptions, the IRS crap, the Secret Service, the Benghazi video lie, the EPA emails, and God knows what else, how come he walks away unscathed? Because his friends in the media go out of their way to not pursue stories (then mock those fellow reporters who do pursue them), in order to protect him. Call the media Obama's scandal condom. It's simple, memorable. And accurate, sadly. I like to think I'm the guy who keeps poking holes in the rubber with a needle.

*"Telling a Democrat not to cry racism is like telling Lynyrd Skynyrd not to play 'Free Bird.'"*
Comparing knee-jerk libs to a band playing its biggest hit makes sense—because when the Democrats play the race card, it gets their people on their feet to cheer that reliable hit. If you don't like Obama's policies, you're racist. If you think Obamacare is a bust,

you're racist. If you think Eric Holder was incompetent, you're racist. In fact . . .

*"When it comes to the race card, the media deals it
like a methed-up blackjack dealer."*
Tip: a metaphor that conjures up a mental image is
almost always effective.

And how to explain Obama's antipathy toward Fox
News while the rest of the media fawns over him?

*"Obama whining about Fox News is like a football
player bad-mouthing the only cheerleader who won't
sleep with him."*
This simile implicates the rest of the media for being
harem members for the president, and it captures
the adolescent angst of our president, born from not
getting everything he wants. I mean, he could be fine
with banging CNN, MSNBC, the *New York Times,
Boston Globe, Huffington Post* . . . but he couldn't
make it with Fox News. And that drives him nuts.
We're like that one playmate who refused to sleep
with Hefner (and it weighs on him daily).

*"Progressives are like Doritos. You eat one, and
Harvard turns out a whole new bag, and they still
make you sick."*
Colleges continue to turn out liberals, because after
all, they're all liberals. It's a conveyor belt of crack-
pottery. Like Doritos, there's never a shortage. And

like Doritos, touching Harvard students leaves weird yellow stuff on your fingers.

## NAME-CALLING

An important part of arguing is calling your opponent a name. The problem is that name-calling is often trite and wordy. If you're going to call somebody a name, make it short and sweet; the shorter the sweeter. "You're an airhead and should be fired" is eight syllables. You can take a nap in eight syllables. Try "Susan Rice" instead—or one of these:

| IF YOU WANT TO SAY | CALL THEM THIS NAME |
| --- | --- |
| You make less sense than Rosie O'Donnell. | Hillary Clinton |
| You're starting to look like a science project. | Bernie Sanders |
| You look like a homeless old man who got in a fight with a passing hubcap. | Harry Reid |
| You had me in a coma at "hello." | Elizabeth Warren |

# 19

# SAY JUNK THAT
# PEOPLE REMEMBER

The goal here is to create a sentence that packs more wisdom in less space. It's what we used to call a "maxim." Philosophers made their living off them, back when philosophers made a living. Another profession killed by cheap labor.

When I say something on *The Five,* during the following commercial break I'll go to Twitter to see if it pulls a response. It's a TV anchor's video game. I say something and see what kind of score it gets. Will fifty people quote it? Seventy-five? Or just some dude name Wilber who keeps sending death threats in ALL-CAPS (and who looks in his Twitter avatar suspiciously like Lou Dobbs)? Twitter is a fishnet that captures responses, which then inform me on what makes for a memorable maxim. I use it as a Gallup poll on how well my synapses are firing that day.

Brevity requires a lot of preparation. Anyone can explain gun rights and drug legalization in a few paragraphs—but can you name that tune in three seconds?

I spent ten years writing cover lines for magazines—those bold declarations meant to persuade you to fork out five bucks and buy something very similar to the thing you bought a month ago. This is no different.

What follows are a number of complex topics, and examples of ways that I've boiled them down. Let's start with this one. It's . . . **All you need to say about:**

### 1. *Guns*

*"The length of a gun attack is dictated by the time it takes for another gun to end it."*
A simple declarative sentence, declaring why gun-free zones are dangerous. A gun that's already present is better than a gun that shows up later. I got that tidbit from John Lott Jr.

*"That celebrity telling you the Second Amendment is dangerous is the same celebrity who has an armed bodyguard."*
This exposes the hypocrisy of media types who claim to be against guns while being protected by men who have them strapped to their waists. Or ankles (which is much sexier).

*"Given the choice, felons would rather target the unarmed over the armed."*
Even the criminal mind understands the value of the Second Amendment. It also explains how gun control is always to the thug's advantage. It's also a hyperdense neutron star of common sense.

## 2. *Drugs*

*"More people have died from the war on drugs than from the drugs themselves."*

If you calculate people murdered worldwide over drugs—on both sides of the law—it crushes drug overdoses. Hell, no one has yet to die from a pot overdose, and I know at least five *Red Eye* guests who keep trying.

*"Drugs don't climb into that bong—much the same way guns don't shoot without a finger."*

We must be against the silly demonization of inanimate objects. We know it's people who kill people, and guns are value-neutral devices. If you agree with that, then you must also agree that it's people who do drugs, not vice versa—and therefore drugs are value neutral. People do drugs because drugs are good.

In fact, drugs are the only substances on the planet that deliver what they promise. That's the weird irony of the world. We legalize the useless (see almost anything we call "over the counter"), then overly regulate the useful (painkillers), and ban the powerful (pot, coke, heroin, DDT).

## 3. *Identity Politics*

*"You can't spell 'assimilate' without 'Islam.'"*

Why do some people immigrate to a country, then refuse to embrace its customs, and instead bring remnants from a place they seek to escape? Why not just stay where you are and cultivate your brand of hell without ruining our fun? It's like a battered spouse leaving her husband to start a "beat-me-in-the-face night" at the Hilton. No one escapes prison and then bunks with the same psycho convict he was forced to share a cell with for twenty years. You escaped—celebrate it! We'll bring the tzatziki.

*"Students are consumed more by identity than by industry."*

They would rather whine than work, because whining brings attention, and work is hard. And often unattended. Identify the problem: a need for identity to feed a ravenous ego.

When faced with someone who is focused only on their sexual identity, their gender, their race, it's important not to mock them, but to ask them why being something is more important than doing something. Realize that you played no constructive role in this identity you are proud of—pride can only come from accomplishment, not by luck or biology. After all, I have amazing blue eyes, but I did not make them. But I have awesome pectoral muscles, and yes, I made those. So I don't brag about my blue eyes, but for a small price I will flex for you.

## 4. *The Military*

*"Saying it's not our fight is why there are more fights."*

When you constantly telegraph to the rest of the world that you're no longer the world's well-armed referee, the thugs take it as a green flag to invade, rape, and pillage. While most things aren't our fight, the ones that are prevent the others. And they have to be fought all-out, with full commitment from Washington (a town that can never get far enough away from any fighting, incidentally).

President Obama has never been interested in winning wars—only in ending them. Why not do both? In fact, there is no point to ending a war if it's not in victory. Obama must have slept through that part of history class (I did, too, but I caught up later with Wikipedia). Fact is, we live under an administration that sees winning only as a strategy for elections, and that has severely compromised our role globally. If America sees no value in victory, that's very unlike our adversaries, who enjoy amassing trophies. Putin would not have gone shopping for land in Eastern Europe if he knew we were up for the fight. Putin's best friend in the world is Obama—they're the yin and yang of politics. Putin takes and takes; Obama's in the kitchen making low-fat brownies. Speaking of . . .

## 5. *President Obama*

*"You don't bring a pet rock to a gun fight, and you certainly don't bring a community organizer to a KGB fight."*

Especially a community organizer on vacation. It's true: President Obama is everywhere you're not. And it's almost always when you need leadership most. He's the guy texting his girlfriend while driving—

eyes not on the road—about to hit a deer. We are that deer.

## 6. *Politics*

*"Politics is a game that bad people play while good people aren't looking."*

Do not expect anything uplifting from politics. When there is tragedy, someone plays politics. Ebola becomes a football for Obama-haters, and for Republican-loathers. Politics is the engine that guarantees your tax money goes for horrible things. Politics enables the corrupt to stay in power, and the greedy to keep gobbling up perks and profits. In short, the only way politicians succeed is if you're busy doing something else. And we are all busy doing something else, because we are normal, decent people. (You must be—you're reading this book.)

In a way, we are all low-information voters, because we have better things to do. There's drinking, sex, and drinking, and sex. And oh yeah, creamed spinach.

But at some point we have to start paying attention (especially to your own local politics, where you *can* do something) and, more important, get others to pay attention. Which is the point here, at page 174 (it's really been a breeze so far).

## FOUR PERSUASIVE POINTS:
## THE PLANNED PARENTHOOD VIDEOS

### How to Explain Evil in Under Five Minutes

**Point One:** When the argument for selling "fetal tissue" begins with "it's a shame to let it go to waste," it destroys the moral case for abortion. By admitting that it's a shame that it's being wasted suggests strongly that you believe that child is/was of value. You reveal that you know what was killed had value.

Only something of value can be wasted, unless you view unborn children as a form of recycling. (Which is the real ugly truth here: in the old days, adults existed to take care of children—to increase the baby's chance of survival. Now it's the reverse: adults use children to enhance their survival through medical "research.")

Perhaps, in the near future, there will be recycling bins located next to the traditional boxes, marked "Paper" and "Glass." We'd likely label it "medical waste," but "victims" would save time and ink.

**Point Two:** Fetal dismemberment cannot be placed under the "pro-choice" umbrella. It was never discussed in *Roe vs. Wade,* or elsewhere. Now, I've accepted that abortion isn't going anywhere. But how does that excuse the ghoulish behavior exposed in those Planned Parenthood videos, revealing their cold, calculated use of organs and parts belonging to unborn children? Pro-choice doesn't mean women have the "choice" to dismember what's discarded. And if you

*(continued)*

175

justify dismemberment by saying it offers the woman solace in knowing that her abortion isn't wasted—well, *you're back to point one, aren't you?*

If dismemberment of a fetus is a right, then so is a right that I possess, allowing me to dissect my uncle after he passed away, too. His skull would make a great paperweight.

**Point Three:** If this baby butchering is perfectly normal activity, why the need for euphemism? Listening to apologists refer to the slicing of dead babies as "fetal research" reveals how evil can only operate under the protective umbrellas of euphemism. What if we experimented on the corpses of death-row dwellers? We'd call it "inmate research," and we'd be vilified. It's an argument one could use on the "research" done on concentration camp victims. And perhaps, in this day and age, we would.

**Point Four:** Much of the media accused the group behind these gotcha videos of selectively editing them to make PP appear worse than they really are. Fact is, the videos were made available, in full, online, the moment they were released. But the real point is this: You can always tell something about someone's choice of outrage. When the media is more upset about the splicing of film than the splicing of babies, it reveals that their reservoir of compassion is as empty as their platitudes about choice. I'd tell them to go to hell, but they're already in it.

# 20

# THREE THINGS ALWAYS
# BEAT TWO THINGS

Unless you're the beneficiary of media welfare (any left-ist with a microphone) you will always be expected to back up the point you're making with examples. Having one example is okay, but no great shakes. Having two examples only illustrates that you have one, plus another one. But having three? That means there are many more! I have no idea why. But it works.

Giving three reasons why you deserve a raise (here's what I've done; here's what I want to do to make my increase worthwhile; I've had offers) tends to be ideally persuasive. And if I'm wrong, it's only because the three reasons you gave were patently false, and also maybe you should get your teeth fixed.

I suppose this even works in fights. Showing up with two friends is better than showing up with none. And it's scarier than just you and one other guy (especially if the other guy is me). Four guys, however—is a "posse," which makes you an "asshole." See the movie *Entourage*. Wait—don't see it.

Try it out here:

### CLIMATE CHANGE

There's plenty of evidence at your fingertips but focus on the most obvious of exaggerations, and have the facts ready (which they will, of course, dispose of).

* Polar bears: Remember when they told us polar bears are disappearing? They aren't. They are multiplying. In fact, I've seen several in my neighborhood, driving Priuses.

* Has it gotten hotter? No. We're in the midst of a sixteen-year pause that may extend for another twenty years or so. That's thirty-six years, the longest decline since Ally Sheedy.

* The big problem with the climate change agenda: it's baked into a crazier mission to handicap America's economic system, by recasting industrial progress that's saved millions of lives as an attack on earth.

Feel free to bring up the bogus hockey-stick theory, or the faulty data from the Brits, or the other assorted lies about consensus—but three should be fine. They're just the tip of the iceberg that still hasn't melted.

## WIN IN THREE

### How to Defend a Pipeline

The key argument against the Keystone pipeline is that it's unsafe. Respond as follows:

1. What's wrong with pipelines? You want oil transported by trains, planes, or buses? That seems kind of weird. What if they crash?

2. If trains and planes and buses are safer than pipelines, we'll need to rethink indoor plumbing. I mean—talk about hazardous waste—we have tons of shit flowing underground that I suppose we're gonna need to bring aboveground. That's gonna smell delicious! Perhaps Uber should start a new line of free transport called Poober.

3. If you're against the pipeline, what about all pipes? Where do we draw the line? If pipes are unsafe, how will radicals make bombs? If pipes were banned, Bill Ayers never would have made tenure!

## Fracking

Fracking gets a bad rap because it's an easy rap to fake, and also because it's a funny word. But it's also an argument you can win, with the variation of the three-step rule.

Fracking can actually save the United States in three easy steps: by making energy cheaper (which is happening

## HOW TO EXPLAIN RISK TO IDIOTS

Everything revolutionary in life starts out as a tad unsafe and then evolves toward better safety over time. It's trial and error, with blood. The first person who tried anything probably died during it. We establish risk, then we reduce risk. But we can never eliminate risk. But isn't relying on lunatic regimes stuck in the seventh century a lot riskier? Here are fifteen things that started awful but through repetition and correction became safer, and better:

- childbirth
- construction
- travel
- fire
- surgery of any kind
- energy extraction
- cooking
- mating with assorted woodland creatures
- most sports
- eating mushrooms
- animal domestication
- dating a musician
- purchasing a used WaterPik at a garage sale
- going to the local ER to get the used WaterPik removed

now), by providing jobs where before there were far fewer (see North Dakota and Pennsylvania, to start), and by getting us away from relying on tyrants and thugs around the world for our fuel (the collapse of the Russian ruble and the Venezuelan economy included).

No doubt someone will confront you with the "But it's not safe" line. Make sure to ask for specifics, which can be easily debunked. But have your facts ready, meaning the latest research revealing that fracking is safe. All can be located using this "Google" thing I found.

Of course, typing in "fracking safety" will only get mostly antifracking sites. (Google is like that, for some reason. Imagine if you googled "Google" and got nothing but "Google sucks" sites. That's how most industries are treated by this lefty conglomerate that is bigger than U.S. Steel but just can't get behind the whole "capitalism" thing.)

So I'll help you. The most common criticism is that the "deep-injected fluids" used in fracking will get into the groundwater, and then we'll all die. So let's pull from what I consider an objective source, *Popular Mechanics,* which states it rather simply: this is "mostly false." "Basic geology prevents such contamination from starting below ground. A fracture caused by the drilling process would have to extend through the several thousand feet of rock that separate deep shale gas deposits from freshwater aquifers."

Basically the intervening layers of rock prevent such breaks from stretching up toward the surface. The magazine uses this simile, from an expert:

"It would be like stacking a dozen bricks on top of each other . . . and expecting a crack in the bottom brick to extend all the way to the top one."

I don't understand this crap. But that's the point. Your ignorance, and my ignorance, enable people dumber than both of us to succeed in preventing one of the great energy revolutions of our time. A revolution conceived by people much smarter than both of us.

## Gun Control

Most arguments for gun control are emotional, which is understandable. People die. The blood. The bodies. It's grim. Guns are bad.

It's an observation more than an (awful) argument, but still a powerful one. A locked-down school, splattered in crimson, beats any well-reasoned, fact-based response in a heartbeat. Which is why, as a pro–Second Amendment guy, you gotta shut up awhile and let the emotions unfold. Political opportunists on Twitter and cable and elsewhere will come along and in a week exhaust their limited repertoire of outrage. That's when you emerge and give them three simple facts:

* Home invasions are fewer in states with more permissive gun laws.

* Felons avoid people with guns, and places where guns are welcome.

* Gun-free zones are enticing to spree killers as targets because these lunatics know they can achieve a higher body count, which is the whole point.

It's true: guns do kill people. But guns also kill murderous people with guns. Just not often enough, alas. Until we do something to effectively and humanely house crazy folks, you're stuck with SIG Sauer.

## Tax Increases on Businesses

Most arguments for increasing taxes break down into two camps:

* Why not! Those rich bastards can afford it!
* I'm not rich, so it's not my problem.

Most proponents of higher taxes automatically assume the extra money is necessary to run the government—that it goes to actual stuff, and that tax increases affect only the rich. That's wrong on all fronts. But this is a small book, so let's focus on three commonsense responses to the cry for higher taxes.

* What happened to the money you already took from me? What happened to that last trillion? The problem has never been about revenue, it's been about spending. If the government actually knew that their funds were limited, they would treat your wallet with respect. Instead, they call the death tax an estate tax, just so they can tax the money not once (it was previously taxed if your mom or dad earned it) but twice. Evil.

* Higher taxes hurt the generators of such taxes. Meaning, the more you penalize, the less the penalized can produce . . . which inevitably reduces the tax base. Because taxpayers move away. Usually to my apart-

ment. I don't mind (I love company). The government treats your money like an invisible roll of toilet paper. They continue to use it on crap because they never know when it runs out. Or care.

* Taxes, combined with regulation, prevent people from taking risks. Fewer businesses open, fewer jobs are available, and all you're left with is Detroit—which you can now purchase with six crates of S&H Green Stamps, and actually get change.

# 21

# USE YOUR MOM

In the early 1990s, on the desk in my office on the Emmaus, Pennsylvania, campus of Rodale Press, sat a single picture. It was of my mother, Jackie.

I had it there not simply because I love (and loved) her—which of course I do (and did). But it served as a guide—one that forced me to simplify anything that required simplification. As an editor for *Prevention* magazine, whenever I had to write about a complicated issue, I would look at the picture and try to figure out how I might explain the topic to her . . . over the phone.

Coronary stents? They're basically straws from a drink you place in the arteries to keep them open for people clogged up with heart disease. They're two-for-one at happy hour!

When I wasn't on the phone with my mom, I would pretend I was having this conversation, to help me explain whatever I was talking about, be it stents, statins, or now, in 2015, crap like sequestration. (I have these conversations aloud, often on public transportation. My fellow New Yorkers seem to enjoy it, and learn so much!)

Sequestration—even the word makes my head hurt. But I am paid to have an opinion, and having an opinion requires that I first understand what the hell I'm talking about, and also that I am able to coherently explain the topic at hand. If I cannot explain sequestration to my mother, then good luck explaining it to you, who doesn't have a mother's patience.

"Hi, Mom, how ya doing."

"Good, honey. What are you going to talk about on *The Five* today?"

"Sequestration."

"Sounds awful!"

"All it means is a law or something like a law that limits the size of the federal budget—the money our government can spend. It's like a credit card limit. But if the government goes over that limit, an alarm goes off and spending cuts are imposed. The whole point is to stop the spending until you can figure out what to do next. We do this because politicians are idiots, and we are idiots for voting for them."

The world of health journalism employs jargon, often used either to impress or to confuse you. Jargon is the Antichrist to persuasion. People who use it should be shot, or forced to read Thomas Pynchon. I prefer to use simple words people have heard before. It's not hard for me. Somehow parading my stupidity just comes naturally.

Once you've learned to be simple, you can be clever. But be too clever and you lose your audience, or they want to strangle you. Anyone watching me on *The Five* has experienced the urge.

## Example One: Immigration

Let's say the argument begins with, "I can't vote for a Republican because they're against immigration."

How do you respond? Simplify. "Please come, but get in line."

Everyone gets the concept of a line and everyone hates line cutters. You aren't against immigration, you are against *illegal* immigration. All you're asking for is a proper process that helps people get into the country easily and without hassle, in a desirable order.

That is not a conservative position: that is a sensible position. And to appeal to liberals, it is also a "fair" position. *Cutting in line is not fair.*

---

### THE SYSTEM IS BROKEN!

You know a lib is about to destroy something when he announces it's broken. "The immigration system is broken," the president will declare, right before he smashes it to pieces—announcing his executive order declaring amnesty for millions. Essentially, he's the handyman you call to fix your garage door, who then claims it's fixed—after removing the door and selling it to the Taliban. After a lib says something is broken, they present a strategy to break it even more. Then they put a bow on it and call it a present.

## Example Two: Legalization of Drugs

Imagine trying to convince your mother or grandmother that legalization of drugs is better than criminalization. Moms would not understand this. It'd be like trying to explain hedge fund derivatives or basic hygiene to Russell Brand. Good luck. Even as a supporter of decriminalization, I get and respect the opposition. Let's face it—drug addicts suck. They suck the life out of families and societies. Some of us just have a different ideas about how to deal with these people. (I want to employ them as throw pillows.)

Do you remember the *Dragnet* episode where the guy on drugs is licking paint off a brush? That one scene alone terrified me. I swore to myself I'd never take drugs—an easy thing to do when you're nine years old. At eighteen, I'd already violated that oath more times than I could count (because I *couldn't* count, thanks to the drugs and the ingestion of paint).

My simplest argument: once it's legal, behavior can be seen and therefore shamed and/or reduced accordingly. Drug addicts are hidden; drunks aren't. And that allows you to kick drunks off your premises (please, be gentle).

Consider Prohibition. Because booze was illegal, it was made illegally (bathtub gin), and it was dangerous and often of dubious quality and proof—people died because they had no idea what they were drinking. Legalizing booze made it quantifiable as a safer, measured product—and the world did not end. People drank responsibly. But those who didn't? Well, they became the town drunks. Likewise with pot. Obvious abusers will be on street corners, licking paintbrushes. The less obvious will be on their couches, licking what's left of their ambition. That's their choice. Shame on them.

And remember, although potheads are annoying, drunks are worse. Men and women who drink too much are often violent, and drive horribly. Pot smokers are silly but mostly benign, and as drivers, research suggests, their impairment is less compared to that of drunks. (Still, it's wrong to drive stoned.)

The problem with drugs is the drug users themselves. Often playing up the novelty of their habits, they do themselves no favors. Snoop Dogg is really this generation's Foster Brooks, a comedian whose entire shtick was playing a drunk (proving he was less versatile than even Charlie Callas). Over time, however, such things change, as illegal behaviors become mundane with legalization. Drunks aren't mysterious—they're tedious. Boring. This will happen with drug users. We just have to give them that chance.

So, in sum, what would I tell my mom? I'd suggest banning her martini. (I'd end up with bruises.)

## Example Three: E-Cigarettes

As a user, and a proponent of their use—I get asked a lot about e-cigs. In short, it's vapor without the usual bad stuff—like tar, and other assorted yucky chemicals that can end your life at an early age. It's not perfect, but the problem is, it still looks like smoking and pisses off people who somehow get angry when they see other people having a good time. It's like trying to keep someone from driving because they had three Shirley Temples.

To explain why the recent attempts to ban vaping are bad, you need to make it clear that this suppression is actually murderous. It's pretty simple: vaping replaces cigarettes, without most of the toxins. The people who give up cigarettes for e-cigarettes therefore are maintaining something enjoyable without the majority of detriments. They are actually going to live longer with this ersatz habit. It's almost the equivalent of drinking water that looks like ethanol instead of drinking ethanol.

This is the answer every doctor has been waiting for: a nicotine delivery device that effectively mimics cigarettes. It's likely no different from a nicotine patch (which no one cares about), or nicotine gum (which no one cares about), and it's better than some popular prescriptions (it doesn't give you crazy nightmares that are often indistinguishable from real life—a drawback when you have a daily show, but a hoot otherwise).

The simplest way to put it: vaping is nicotine gum that you inhale. And anyone who opposes that should oppose gum, too. (And Shirley Temples.)

# 22

# BE COLUMBO

At *Prevention* and *Men's Health,* much of my work entailed the brutal challenge of interviewing doctors—aloof but brilliant creatures possessing two disadvantages. They were not press-friendly, and they didn't know how to articulate the fine work they actually do.

That was the irony in the world of health: the bizarre health nuts and quacks were ace at selling you the most ridiculous things, while a respectable MD, whose work involves carefully quantifying the results of scientific repetition, and publishing the results of such careful repetition, cannot sell you his achievements or persuade you of his findings to save his own life or your own. It's beneath him, and he has no interest in it. And if you don't understand what he does, that's your problem. Literally, if you need treatment.

Does this sound familiar? The hucksters are great at

191

selling, and the experienced substantive folks come off as stiff and clunky? It's our political system, channeled through the *New York Times* and its clingy minions. The left can sell bad ideas; the right can't sell a decent one. The left can convince you a bad idea that killed millions should be reanimated (see: communism and socialism). The right can look at their victories of the past and fail to tell you why they were victorious, and why it mattered.

The scourge of health and science writing is the desire for a sellable answer. The fact is, like Lil' Kim's face, science is never settled, and is always changing. But answers raise money for grants, sell magazines, and grab eyeballs for your inane talk show.

The problem: although science is messy and hard, the media hacks will shape it into something simple and alluring by leaving certain things out. Lawyers call it "willful blindness," but it's simply "stupidity."

As a writer whose role was to interview cranky doctors, it was my job to ask them simple questions, and get simple answers, and read the studies they authored. And then simplify everything.

The key to getting started is never to be afraid of admitting you're stupid. Because pretending to know more than you know always ends in disaster. If someone asks you if you can fly a plane, you don't say yes if the answer is no (especially if you are settling into the pilot's seat). Oddly, we do this when discussing almost anything complex.

Stupidity opens doorways to knowledge and invites experts to teach you for free.

Here is the wrong way to approach any conflict: you

come to it loaded with jargon you barely understand, hoping to impress. You will get nowhere.

The right way is to start it off by saying you know nothing. Chances are whoever you're talking to will be so shocked by your refreshing honesty, he'll walk you through an entire issue with glee. He might even give you a warm hug (no tongue). And he'll like the fact that you're coming to him for help.

I did this in my previous incarnations at health mags: I told every doctor that I knew nothing. "Doctor," I would say, "before we discuss Alzheimer's, who the heck is Alzheimer?"

That opens the doorway to a methodical explanation of the history of the disease.

I've asked doctors millions of dumb questions (a specialty of mine), starting every interview with "I'm just a reporter, and forgive me if I embarrass myself, but could you explain . . ."

I stole all of this from Columbo. The legendary television detective mastered the art of asking seemingly dumb, apologetic questions . . . until the very end of the ninety-minute episode when he nailed the perp (usually played by William Shatner or Jack Cassidy).

All you're really doing is asking questions that no one dares to ask because they're all too scared to look stupid.

### Example One: Amnesty

Every Democrat seems to be for this thing. And also a few Republicans.

Why? I mean, if it's so great, why do we even need to

declare it? From what I can tell, there seems to be absolutely no downside!

Pardon me for being stupid, but if amnesty is a good thing, then this "border" thing must be a bad thing. *So, are borders a bad thing?*

If borders aren't a bad thing . . . then I'm confused. Because we're saying it's okay to come here illegally. Can you explain to me how you can have a border and not be against amnesty? The dumb question "Why do we have a border?" leads to the smarter debate over law and order. And often to fisticuffs and bail hearings.

## Example Two: Birth Control

As I write this, activists are demanding that Fordham University pay for students' condoms. A casual observer might say, "Why not? Students need condoms." They sure do—to ensure we don't make any more of these Fordham students. The problem is, Fordham is a Jesuit college, so it's not exactly part of the school's belief system. But more important, the activists are calling it a human right—yes, finally, condoms are a human right. You can laugh, or you can be inquisitive and ask them to explain their stance.

How are condoms a human right? If condoms are a human right that must be paid for by someone else, why not your food or clothing? Aren't those two items more important than condoms?

What's a human right? Is it something that you demand another human pays for? What if I, a Jesuit, do not want to pay for your condoms—isn't that *my* human right?

Simple questions open doors to smart thoughts, and prevent your opponent from avoiding coherent explanations in favor of strident emotion.

And by the way, this technique works even better if you can do it in Columbo's voice. Now there's a man who never paid for someone else's condoms.

Besides, if condoms really are a human right, wouldn't Thomas Jefferson have included them in the Declaration of Independence? (Although I read that Ben Franklin might have tried.)

# ★ ★ ★ **23** ★ ★ ★

# CROSS-DRESS

In order to win, many Democrats will put on costumes to appear less like a Democrat.

Which raises a question: if you need to pretend to be a Republican to win elections, why not just be a Republican at all times? Why be a liberal, then turn right to ensure survival?

Because the media won't allow it.

Democrats are slaves to political correctness because they know they will be crucified if they are not (they see it happen to the Republicans they secretly agree with). They placated the media police, and now they live in the jail they built.

When liberals need to win over voters, they change. Suddenly common sense erupts like a reality geyser.

They embrace coal. They talk tough on crime. They talk about jobs, national security, Iran, and other stuff that matters.

And the media gets it, and plays along—the same way they always do when libs lie. (See Obama and his phony denial about gay marriage. Or rather, *don't* see it. Because, unless you go looking very hard for it, you're unlikely to find it. That's another thing the left is good at disguising: history.)

What does it tell you that the Democrats are the only party that needs a disguise to win? It tells you that they're smart enough to know they suck. And that's pretty damn smart, if you ask me.

For they realize that in times of crisis, you must become a conservative. Conservatives, after all, are interested in conserving what they have. Liberals are romanced by risk. As I've said, one can be a liberal only in periods of calm. But when the going gets rough, every damn conservative value becomes necessary: security, suspicion, safety, guns, a distrust of kale. It was amazing how many liberals sounded like conservatives when Ebola or ISIS arrived. Liberals, aware that their ideology is fundamentally useless in times of strife, switch when it matters. There were very few "progressive" matters in Congress on 9/12.

Then conservatives dive in and help (see Reagan after Carter). We do our thing—straighten shit up—until the media calls us callous and cold, and in comes another liberal. This cycle has been going on since there were dinosaurs (which is, like, well over a thousand years ago!). The luxury of calm leads to amnesia, then chaos.

You're seeing this play out now as law enforcement comes under attack by the left. After decades of dramatic reductions in crime, the police have become victims of their own success. No one remembers how bad things were, especially if you got conked on the head and robbed back in 1993. In which case your memory is probably shot anyway.

So if liberals can cross-dress so easily, without getting an actual sex change . . . why can't conservatives? Why can't we wear a costume to win votes? Bait and switch!

It's time to do the same thing. Let's make Halloween every day and pretend. Use their language to make your case. It will leave them speechless.

That means, if you're a Republican, you might at times need to slip into the bullshit costume, while winking to your voters. That means . . . lying.

And enjoying every minute of it.

---

### THREE TO WIN

How to become a liberal in three easy steps:

1. Care. About anything. Just say, "I care."

2. Say we need to "tackle" the problem. It's the only tackling that the left finds acceptable.

3. Out-concern them. When they say something is bad, say, "It's actually worse." Extra points if you say the problem is "systemic."

---

## FORGET THE SECOND AMENDMENT, IT'S CLASS WARFARE

Rather than saying owning a gun is as fundamental as breathing, embrace precaution, responsibility. Agree with concerns of the antigun lobby: note that it's refreshing that liberals care about *your* rights as a gun owner.

Invite them shooting. If they refuse, ask them how they can judge something they refuse to experience. Refusing such an offer is bigoted, frankly. It's like refusing to enter a mosque! Or enjoying ethnic food! Or eating kebabs in a mosque! What happened to your open-mindedness? After all, black people shoot guns too! You won't come to the range? What are you—racist?

Fact: There will never be a realized version of gun control, because it's actually gun confiscation. If nothing else, that is an unconstitutional taking. It's more or less the legal equivalent of an unwarranted public domain action (I know this not because I'm a lawyer, but because I saw an episode about it on *The Good Wife*). And they know it. So let liberals feel some progress, pat them on the head, and everything will be fine.

## Call It What It Is

| WHAT IT'S CALLED | WHAT YOU CALL IT |
| --- | --- |
| gun control | misogyny |
| birth control | girl control |
| global warming | starvation reduction |
| militarization | fashion smarts |
| amnesty | cheating |

# IT'S NOT RACISM, IT'S ASSHOLES

* Admit that racism not only existed, but still exists
(not a lie, this is true: we have 317 million people . . .
I'm willing to guess at least a million or so are racist
jackasses). And then ask your opponents if their solution for reducing racism is anything superior to the
NYPD's, a minority-driven majority that has reduced
black death substantially. The NYPD has done more
for young blacks than Al Sharpton, Maxine Waters,
*In Living Color,* and the Wu-Tang Clan combined.

However, you can't simply tell Al Sharpton he sucks
and expect him to listen (not unless you are paying him to
listen). Here I am pessimistic: so many people involved in
these contemporary race wars do not want a solution. The
conflict is too profitable, and race has become a conduit for
revolution—in some cases, a violent one. What could not
be accomplished through Occupy Wall Street is now being
funneled through Ferguson. And a person who wants cops
dead is no person you should be debating anyway. Which
means you should avoid career social-justice agitators, or
anyone with tenure and a ponytail.

## GOOD NEWS IS BAD NEWS

Liberals hate good news. Think about it. Who *loses* if this simple truth is uttered: liberal or conservative? Fill in the blanks below with one of those two choices.

1. Things are getting better for blacks in America.

   _____

2. We're making the rivers cleaner.

   _____

3. We have more trees in America than ever.

   _____

4. According to the numbers, we don't have to keep pouring money into school programs that are really welfare deals.

   _____

5. Higher temperatures save lives.

   _____

6. The polar bears are fine.

   _____

7. The majority of NYPD officers are minorities.

   _____

8. Domestic production is making us less dependent on foreign oil and foreign tyrants.

   _____

# IF YOU DENY RADICAL ISLAM, THEN YOU ARE A RACIST!

Always condemn those who are bigoted against Muslims. Then ask how your adversaries feel about a set of *ideas,* not a set of *people.* Can one be bigoted against a set of ideas? If they say yes, they're conflating extremism with Islam— making themselves the bigots.

One can love Muslims but hate tenets of Islam that are shitty to women, gays, and nonbelievers. Despising jihad and fatwas does not make one a bigot. For they are ideas, not races. If your adversary thinks that's the case, then he is the actual bigot, for he believes condemning fatwas is the same as condemning Islam. Mildly chastise him for not being able to separate Muslims from the hate espoused in various Islamic factions. And for not sticking up for women, gays, and nonbelievers. Tell him that his narrow-mindedness depresses you. "Oh, evolve!" you say. Then sit back and watch the cognitive dissonance commence.

# YES, SEXISM IS BAD, BUT WHO'S THE WORST AT IT?

Sexism exists. For example, a current study shows women prefer male bosses over female. How sexist is that? It's terrible. How do we force women to change their minds? Should we? I mean, if we try to convince women that men aren't better bosses, even though they feel that way, isn't that sexist, too? Why can't we take women at their word?

Sexism must be tackled at its root—and these sexist women must be stopped. They should be fired! Oh wait.

And what about women who get enraged over criticism of female candidates, celebrities, and so on, but never when similar criticism is directed at men? This sexism—a belief that women are incapable of withstanding criticism— must be stopped. It is only when women can handle the brutal criticism that men face every day, without defense from those who believe women are weak, that we will have reached true equality. Stop coddling these women! It's so sexist!

# ★ ★ ★ 24 ★ ★ ★

# FILL-INS FOR LIBERALS

The "if it were Bush" argument already seems horribly tired, this is true—but that's because it suffers from no rebuttal. That point exists precisely because it cannot be refuted. So you can keep using it over and over, because it's correct. The only problem now is, what was once timely and incisive has become very boring.

Even when I use this argument, I get sick of hearing my own voice (you can imagine how my wife feels). "Yes, but if this had happened under Bush, you'd be screaming for impeachment." If I had a buck for every time I've said that, I'd have enough to buy a used Jetta (a 2011 with minimal bloodstains goes for a little over ten grand), which means I've said that a whole lot.

But before we address its overuse, let's admit that it's real. President Obama has gotten away with more shit than a Bronx sewer main—simply because the media is willing to overlook his minor foibles and his major incompetence.

**WHERE YOU SEE OBAMA, BLAME BUSH!**

**(A Tip Sheet for the Establishment Media)**

- The IRS targets and investigates political groups it feels are critical of President Obama.
  *Blame:* Bush for creating an atmosphere in which such cavalier intolerance can occur. The IRS is still recovering from that reckless era.

- The Secret Service scandal erupts under Obama.
  *Blame:* the previous president's frat-boy persona, which allowed this sleaziness to fester.

- A high-level flack under Obama called a world leader "chickenshit."
  *Blame:* Bush for encouraging that Texas-style slang during his eight-year reign. Seriously, you don't pick up that kind of talk at Columbia.

- Under Obama, economic inequality got worse, as the stock market surged past 18,000 (as I write this). The rich got richer. Sorry, not just the rich . . . the really rich.
  *Blame:* President Bush—as a proponent of the evil web that is capitalism and which President Obama has only begun to untangle. We realize that this transformation to a more compassionate model of redistribution could take decades. We may need to elect Michelle, then Chelsea.

He's their favorite child—he never gets grounded, receiving only gratitude for just being himself. And as with any favored child, it has spoiled him.

The media only does their job when there is someone in office who doesn't mirror their progressive assumptions. So even though this cranky complaint appears repetitive, it's only because *they* want you to feel that way. They want you to stop pointing out this fundamental truth because, in their hearts, they know you are right—and they are hypocrites.

The solution is to present their hypocrisy creatively. It's not enough to say, "What if it were Bush?" The real question is, "Why is it okay now . . . and not then?" And leave personalities, that is, the presidents, out of it.

That forces them to reveal the weakness in their beliefs. They cannot face the reality that the Chosen One is really a teacher's pet with a fan club. That the person they had been waiting for actually showed up, and walked all over them—in golf cleats, no less. (Which actually feels pretty good, I'm told.)

## ★ ★ ★ 25 ★ ★ ★

# USE THEIR SILENCE TO
# SPEAK VOLUMES

Priorities expose the differences between left and right. As a righty, you tend toward the big-ticket miseries (as I label them): Islamic terror, tyrants, radical regimes, toxic ideologies, deadly criminals, vicious gangs, romantic comedies. These are just in my neighborhood. But it's part of our genetic makeup, apparently. As conservatives, we tend to make it a priority to protect what we have from the onslaught of evil. It's not a bad priority, in that it really is the only priority. It can make you seem a bit paranoid, like a well-armed hoarder in a panic bunker (me in my retirement years). But let's face it: because of this demeanor, you're the guy everyone is going to flee to for safety. When the world's crumbling, I'm running to my Green Beret buddy's house, not mine. And my house has better wine.

Meanwhile, the left focuses on smaller outrages and infractions (appropriately titled "microaggressions"), and finds an amazing measure of joy and solace in punitive actions. If you say something on Twitter that violates their tender sensitivities, they will do what is necessary to get you to apologize, to get you suspended, to get you fired. This is their form of exercise. This is what brings their lives meaning. Meanwhile, of course, in other countries people are raped, enslaved, executed, beheaded—for simply existing. Only in the greatest country in human history could so many obsess over such marginal offenses. Problem is, the big risks haven't gone away. Not really.

As the old saying goes, the best way to turn liberals into conservatives is to mug them—with reality. Sit them down and go over their priorities. Don't dismiss their priorities; just align them properly so they can see what truly matters.

## KEEP YOUR OUTRAGES STRAIGHT

### It's Not Sexism~It's Racism!

New outrage bubbles up over a word, a joke, a misplaced comma. Recently a woman created a video of herself on the streets of New York, claiming she had been catcalled more than a hundred times in twelve hours. I watched the video. Nearly all the catcalls were "hey" and "nice." The woman seemed to walk in areas where minority men were standing around. She didn't go to Saks or Equinox. In that same month, a woman was stoned to death in the Middle East, with her father leading the execution—for some adulterous infraction. In the same month, Boko Haram had kidnapped and enslaved dozens of women. So, yeah, catcalls suck. But they don't rate, compared to true evil. Unless of course you don't have to worry about primitives like Boko Haram— thanks to evil conservative institutions like the American military and the police. Then "raising catcalling aware- ness" becomes a human rights issue that The Hague should really look into.

## It's Not Tolerance—It's Censorship!

As I write this (drunk and in boxers), a silly controversy brews in Berkeley (yes, redundant, I know). Thousands of people have signed a petition to get Bill Maher's commence- ment speech canceled. The wusses behind the petition are upset over Maher's criticism toward Islam, the only reli- gion, he says, "that acts like the mafia that will fucking kill you if you say the wrong thing, draw the wrong picture, or write the wrong book." He's been called a bigot for this view, by a sweaty Ben Affleck, on his HBO show, which is hilari- ous given that Islam is not a race.

Liberals also continue to demean Christians for adher- ing to their beliefs against gay marriage. These are people who may be wrong—but they aren't beheading anyone over their misconceptions. At least, not since the fifteenth cen- tury. I'd say that's progress. Strange that "progressives" don't appreciate the distinction.

On the left, the folks who are yelling the loudest are the same people usually silent about true religious intolerance around the globe. Remind them that we have Christians being massacred for simply not believing in Islam. We have assorted other religious types (and even Muslims) being slaughtered over doctrinal differences by ISIS.

211

The question you must always ask the liberal: why are you angry about this, and not about that?

The honest answer would be:

**One:** It's easy. You can sign a petition, and still get to the sit-in without really doing anything that strenuous.

**Two:** It's cool. The low-priority outrages—chasing some lunkhead white Christian or an insensitive celebrity—create buzz and attention that you would normally never get elsewhere. It's more fun, too, because everyone the lib knows hates those people.

**Three:** It's safe. Far less dangerous to call out a group of devout Christians than ISIS. It made Marilyn Manson's career. He burned Bibles on tour—but never a Koran. That's actually a compliment for Christians, though the world's saggiest Goth has no idea why.

## It's Not Environmentalism—It's Class Warfare!

Concern for the environment expresses itself in many ways. Almost all of them border on the insanely apocalyptic. The reason: there is no pushback. We've learned that if you want to keep talking without interruption, claim you care for the planet. No one will stop you. Even if you're doing it in traffic, during rush hour. While bowing a cello.

No one bothers to prioritize environmental dangers. Well, almost no one. Bjorn Lomborg does it, but few listen because what he says violates the dogma presented by the panicky priests currently running the climate change religion (also, his name is Bjorn).

What are most climate change crazies silent about?

Lomborg points out that if we agreed to the Kyoto Protocols, it would cost about $150 billion a year (or 120 Hillary Clinton speeches), which he calls "a bad deal" (this from a TED talk back in 2005). As he points out, "All models show it will postpone warming for about six years in 2100. So the guy in Bangladesh who gets a flood in 2100 can wait until 2106." (They're patient, the Bangladeshis.) In sum, "We've spent a lot of money doing a little good."

Lomborg points out that for half that cash, you could solve "all major basic problems in the world." That is, "clean drinking water, sanitation, basic health care, and education." We could even find a cure for Russell Brand.

His key point: free trade. "If we could get free trade, and especially cut subsidies in the U.S. and Europe, we could basically enliven the global economy to an astounding number of about 2,400 billion dollars a year, half of which would accrue to the third world." (The other half would go to Mark Cuban, I suspect.) He says that within five years that could quickly pull some 300 million people out of poverty. Roughly the population of Manhattan.

## Hey Media, Which Is Worse?
## A Jihadist or a Scientologist?

| BENEFIT | JIHADIST | SCIENTOLOGIST |
|---|---|---|
| 1. liberated from painful experiences | beheading | auditing |
| 2. drug-free life | beheading | Narc-Anon |
| 3. fate of women in the religion | stoning | Kirstie Alley |

# ★ ★ ★ 26 ★ ★ ★

# STUNTS

## OR, HOW AN IDIOTIC, ABSURD ACT OF STUPIDITY CAN REVEAL A TRUTH ABOUT LIFE AND OTHER CRAP

I'm no stranger to doing dumb things. In fact, dumb things are some of my best friends. Back in grade school in San Mateo, California, I was suspended for the last two weeks of seventh grade for lighting firecrackers in class. I still have no idea why I did it, but the punishment felt like a reward. They wanted me to stay home, until the next year, when I returned as student body president. It was a win-win, I suppose. I caught up on *The Price Is Right* and *Let's Make a Deal* and drank a lot of my mom's milk shakes (home was a real prison). I'd kill for that life today.

Fast-forward to similar antics that marred my career. When I got canned as editor of *Men's Health* in 2000, I slipped a few lines into the "letter from the editor" of my last issue. The letter was originally about Halloween (it was the October issue), and I added this: "I've just been fired from this job—and I never saw it coming. . . . Dangerous ideas can instill a little fear—and when you scare your boss, you're gone." Rodale Press, which owned the mag, stopped the presses halfway through the print run to remove my simple but honest thoughts (not exactly the "Stop the presses!" moment I'd envisioned for my journalism career). It cost them money, and created some ugly press in the "media" media—which they deserved. I'm sure I cost them more than they saved by firing me. That wasn't my intention, but it does feel sort of just, considering how I'd raised their circulation (along with their blood pressure on more than one occasion).

I'd like to think that from the moment of lighting firecrackers in my St. Gregory's uniform to tossing that final grenade in a magazine, I'd grown a little (about six inches, tops). Yes, "St. Gregory's." There is a career-making psychology dissertation embedded in that, I suspect.

## WHAT MAKES A GOOD PRANK

The stunt must convey a message. It can't simply be something that makes someone look stupid or you look great. Firecrackers are bad, but that editorial grenade . . . good. If there's no reason for your mayhem, then it's simply destructive.

A prank, to prove its worth, must be directed against something that simultaneously has more power than you but is potentially dangerous. Pranking Christians? Please. Try drawing Muhammad, then start bragging.

# HOW TO PERSUADE PEOPLE THAT
# PR LEADERS ARE MORONS

I've told this story before (usually drunk) so I'll keep it short. I was asked to speak at a magazine industry conference about how to create "buzz." I hated the idea. Buzz comes from great work, wit, and effort; a conference on this would be "un-buzzy." So I turned it down. Then I hired "little people" from a friend (I think he likes them in a nonplatonic manner) who arrived with clipboards and phones on vibrate.

To quote the *New York Times:* "As editors from *Rolling Stone, Glamour* and *O: The Oprah Magazine* opined on the serious business of buzz creation, the actors began chomping loudly on handfuls of potato chips as their cellphones started ringing furiously. (The actors, of course, loudly took the calls.)"

When the panelists tried to get these little people to pipe down, they accused the panelists of discrimination against little people. That left them anchorless in an ocean of political correctness. In the media, they finally got nailed for what they had been nailing everyone else for: insensitivity. That was my goal: to hang the PC on their own PC petard (also, to investigate what a "petard" is). And in the process, teach them how to create real "buzz." I was promoted to brand development, which is L.A.-speak for "drinking by the pool, waiting for your dealer."

# HOW TO PERSUADE PEOPLE THAT FASHION LEADERS ARE NAKED EMPERORS

During Men's Fashion Week in New York, as editor of *Stuff,* I was told I had front-row seats to a major show on that Thursday. I had no interest in going, for I loathe the pecking order of the fashion world and the fact that Crocs are no longer in style. It's a grim universe, based on desperate approval from pretentious peers. (Also, I had hockey tickets.)

So when told by my fashion editor that I had to go to this show, I panicked. Then I looked on the floor—where our products manager had left a bearskin rug, complete with the bear head. (I'm not kidding—it was really there. It wasn't a hallucination.) I scooped it up and put it in a bag. Across the street from the fashion show, I sat at a bar and downed three tequila shots, and perhaps ingested some other things—and then went to the bathroom, where I put on my outfit, which was nothing but the bearskin rug. The head rested in between my cheek and shoulder—the face, the claws, the perfectly fanged teeth all present in their grotesque beauty. I showed up to the event in this garish garb, and immediately had every photographer around me, as I was interviewed by legendary fashion editor André Leon Tally about my look, which he found to be beautiful. I ended up being written up in some big-time rags—in which I claimed that the bear had died for a cause. "His name is Skittles . . . and he lived and died, for fashion."

★ ★ ★

The stunt was silly and impulsive, but it revealed how easy it is to trick even the professionals in an industry based on illusion—who had no idea if my garb was authentic or a joke (it was both: it was a real bear, with real teeth and claws). I left a brief but memorable stain on fashion—and left the event feeling awesome that I had accomplished something out of nothing. I think I got lucky that night. In the bear costume, no less. Or maybe it was with the bear costume. It really didn't matter at that point.

The point is, it was a stunt with a purpose: to turn the pretensions of this crowd of lefty poseurs on themselves, to highlight their basic fatuousness. To this day I suspect there are fashion editors out there who still don't realize it was a joke. But that's okay. Far more people realized after this that those editors are the joke.

## HOW TO PERSUADE MUSLIMS THAT GAY PEOPLE NEED LOVE TOO

**Note: If you've already read about this before, my apologies; please skip to page 221.**

Back in August 2010, during the "Ground Zero mosque" outrage, I decided to build New York City's first Islamic-friendly gay bar—right next to the yet-to-be-completed Park51 mosque, which the media had shorthanded to "Ground Zero mosque" because it was mere blocks from the 9/11 graveyard. Per my monologue on *Red Eye:* "As an American, I believe they have every right to build the mosque. Which is why, in the spirit of outreach . . . I'm announcing tonight, that I am planning to open the first gay bar that caters not only to the West, but also to Islamic gay men. I hope the mosque owners will be as open to the bar, as I am to the new mosque."

I later emailed and tweeted the mosque, seeking a response. They tweeted back: "You're free to open whatever you like. If you won't consider the sensibilities of Muslims, you're not going to build dialog."

After that tweet, *Red Eye* cohost Bill Schulz suggested we name the gay bar *Dialogue.*

The stunt took off. Donations were pledged, and it certainly felt like this bar was actually going to happen. Which, to be clear, was not my point. My point, of course, was to expose the developers' hypocrisy in the realm of tolerance. I told the developers that I respected their right to build the mosque, and in return they should respect my right to build a gay bar. Of course, instead they questioned my sensitivity toward their beliefs. Note the irony: did they consider the sensitivity toward New Yorkers when they decided to build the mosque so close to the site?

Of course, some people called me a bigot, but those people missed the point. Shouldn't they champion gay rights before they sling accusations of Islamophobia at me? This stunt exposed a humorless, PC left and introduced a little humor to an otherwise shrill affair, populated on both sides by ideologues and hacks. A prank can cut through all that bullshit.

The bar was never opened. To this day the mosque is still under construction. I guess we'll count it even.

★ ★ ★ **27** ★ ★ ★

# FIND YOUR INNER DRUNK

I believe in mind reading. In fact, I know *for a fact* that it is 100 percent possible to think someone else's thoughts. It happens every day; you just don't notice it.

For example: Let's say you're in an elevator ("you're in an elevator") and an employee you do not know enters from another floor. Do you know what he's thinking? Of course you do.

"I don't know this guy well enough to say hi."

(Unless he's thinking, "This looks like the guy whose picture is hanging in the post office." Either way, you're reading his mind!)

My job is to think your thoughts and then express them eloquently—with force, humor, and verve. But I do not wish to express the obvious thoughts, because then that's

221

too easy. That's simply delivering assumptions, which you can get from just about anyone these days. Especially if you have a TV with cable access.

I prefer to articulate the thoughts you cannot express. Those sitting somewhere in your brain, waiting to be unlocked. How do I get there? How do I access the unspeakable thoughts—so that you will feel a sense of great wonder and satisfaction when you hear them come from someone else's mouth?

I do something that, in my opinion, never fails: I pretend I'm drunk.

I have a theory. If you act drunk, you are drunk. (I have another theory about what caused the extinction of the dinosaurs, but those clowns at the Smithsonian will no longer take my calls.)

If you're looking for a strong, straightforward opinion (that might in fact be right), you'll find it sitting on a bar stool in front of a warm Guinness. The fact is, drunks have an opinion on everything. That's a valuable thing to tap into, especially if you're coming up empty on original ideas.

Just about every day, I do one or two shows. Within that workload, I cover a dozen stories. Each story requires from me an opinion, an idea, an insight. The problem is, I sometimes don't have one. There are topics I simply don't give a shit about (like stories about royalty; especially stories about royalty). But my job is to say something, anything. And I'll be damned if I am going to waste your time with fake bullshit that you hear from other a-holes. I am an a-hole with *real* bullshit, if nothing else.

So I get drunk. Not literally, but figuratively. I sit at my computer and think, "What would drunk Greg say?" Because I know drunk Greg wouldn't shut up about anything. (I know this because bartenders and former friends often reminded me.)

So let's say it's October 2014, and the midterm elections approach. I'm not an expert on this stuff. I couldn't tell you who's leading in North Dakota, who might take Alaska, and if there's a dogfight in the Carolinas (I'm not even sure where these places are, or where I am now). If you asked me point-blank, "Greg, what's your prediction on 2016?" I'd sputter that it's likely to follow 2015.

But then I would conjure up "drunk Greg" and ask myself to answer that question, as if I were drunk. It's pretty easy. Recall the last time you were drunk, how it felt—the looseness, the lack of restraint, the laserlike incoherence!

So if sober Greg has nothing on the midterms, drunk Greg says this: "Who the hell cares if we can't get the White House? If we can't find one single decent Republican president, then we deserve to lose. Now pass me those peanuts, goddammit."

Another complicated example in need of insobriety is the Middle East, a crisis that most of us don't think about until we have to. If I come up blank, I revert to drunk Greg, who always has an opinion. And it would be, about the Middle East: "Three groups all claiming it's their promised land. And we're stuck with them. Who doesn't keep calling you the Great Satan? Hang out with that guy. Also, do you have any weed?"

Speaking of pot legalization.

This is a story that suffers from both catastrophic thinking and rose-colored-glasses-wearing goofs. Fact is, pot isn't as harmless as people say it is, but potheads aren't as harmful as people think they are.

How does drunk Greg respond when someone asks him if legalization is a good thing?

"When was the last time a pothead punched you in the face? In every fucking fight in my life, it's been with drunks. Hell, I once started a fight with myself after drinking tequila for six hours. I kicked my own ass." The case is still in litigation.

# THE GAME AT THE BAR

Here is a psychological experiment.

Put yourself in a crowded bar watching the World Series, watching your favorite team.

The bar is filled equally with fans of both teams.

When the opposing team scores and takes the lead, their fans cheer.

How do you feel? Not simply about the scoring, but about the cheering.

Probably an odd mix of defeatism, anger, and, if you're honest, envy and shame. The scientific term is "pissed off."

Now, imagine your team scoring to retake the lead . . . and you cheer. Loudly. It's as if your reaction is obliterating all those feelings you felt before—just as you sense the defeated emotions around you, as the gang expresses exhilarating, mocking delight.

The emotions in both instances match the same feeling you get in political discourse.

And this happens because such discourse has achieved a competitive intensity. Perhaps this sensation was always this intense, but it seems we're seeing more of it—being in a contentious time where division is no longer a place where a team resides, but a condition stoked by media, academics, and activists.

So, in this bar, how do you conduct yourself, knowing that no matter what you say or do, the other team's fans will never become fans of your team?

Do you cheer more loudly when you score, and do you feel more anger when they score one on you?

For the sake of converting new fans, it makes no difference.

But for the sake of civility and kinship on a crowded planet, it's not such a bad thing to smile when you score, and to smile when you don't. And every now and then, buy a round for your opponents, just so they know you're human, much like them. Assuming you're human, that is.

That way, even if you don't win the arguments or convert the opposition, we'll all have a much better shot at enjoying the game. A game that, for all of us, is far too short, and goes by far too quickly.

# ACKNOWLEDGMENTS *and Crud*

As always, thanks to my wife, Elena, for her bottomless patience and endless support.

As always I must thank everyone who helped me along the way, including all the great folks at Fox News—especially Roger Ailes, whose confidence in me is the highest compliment I've received in my career.

I must also express gratitude to the people who read and shaped this manuscript. My deep thanks go to my editor, Mary Choteborsky; my agent, Jay Mandel; and my manager, Aric Webb. Paul Mauro—thanks for the initial read and thoughts. Denis Boyles—the stern guidance and extra jokes. Dana Perino—the dog pictures (and the camaraderie).

And the late Andrew Breitbart, for reminding me to embrace obstacles.

Because this book is meant to instruct, it had to pull examples from my past. So, to mangle Morrissey, forgive me if you've heard some of this stuff before. I know I've touched on the pranks in previous books, have elaborated on my work history elsewhere. Examples of persuasive arguments were sometimes taken from stuff I've said on *The Five* and *Red Eye,* but also from speeches, appearances, tweets, blog posts, and drunken rants on street corners. If I sound like I'm repeating myself, it's only because I'm repeating myself. I hear that comes with aging. I hear that comes with aging.

And lastly, of course, I must thank my family—and especially my late mother, who passed away in 2014. Every time I get angry, I feel her spirit; and every time I laugh, I feel her joy. Every single day I feel her by my side, which counters the grief of missing her. I know that she made me who I am—and I hope she knows that, too.